PRAISE FOR KONST.
FROM OTHER MEMBERS
OF THE PARANORMAL COMMUNITY

"Konstantinos has impressed me with his knowledge of a wide range of topics related to the unexplained and paranormal. He knows how to ask both the right questions and the tough ones, and filter out the nonsense from what seems to be real."

—Loyd Auerbach, renowned parapsychologist and former consultant for *Criss Angel Mindfreak* on A&E

"There are not enough words in the dictionary to describe the passion Konstantinos has for his work. He is dedicated, caring, and unique."

—Kristyn Gartland, case manager for the Atlantic Paranormal Society (TAPS) and cast member of *Ghost Hunters* on SyFy

"I only got to know Konstantinos recently but have always heard about his work. I consider him to be a very knowledgeable occult expert. I was impressed by his vast knowledge regarding spirit communication."

—Heather Taddy, documentarian for *Paranormal State* on A&E

"Konstantinos has the most amazing way of taking difficult-to-understand topics and shedding light on them for the 'everyday Joe.' He's amazing and a credit to any project he lends his name to."

—Tiffany Johnson, nationally renowned psychic and featured psychic on A&E's *Psychic Kids*

Werewolves

ABOUT THE AUTHOR

Konstantinos (New York) has been a paranormal researcher for nearly two decades. This is his seventh book published by Llewellyn. He has consulted for, and been a guest on, various shows and documentaries on History, MTV, SyFy, NBC, Discovery Channel, and other networks. A onetime physics major, Konstantinos' current project is to explain the paranormal using modern scientific discoveries, especially in the realm of quantum mechanics. He has been a featured speaker at conferences run by the cast of *Ghost Hunters* (SyFy) and the team from *Paranormal State* (A&E). He has also done voice acting for the bestselling videogame *Grand Theft Auto: Vice City*, and was lead vocalist for the band Bell, Book & Candle (Cleopatra Records).

For appearance dates and other information, please see his website: http://www.konstantinos.com

KONSTANTINOS

Werewolves

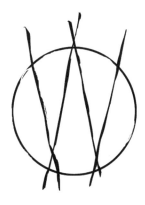

The Occult Truth

Llewellyn Publications
Woodbury, Minnesota

First Edition
First Printing, 2010

Cover design by Kevin R. Brown
Editing by Brett Fechheimer

Llewellyn is a registered trademark of Llewellyn Worldwide Ltd.

Library of Congress Cataloging-in-Publication Data
Konstantinos, 1972–
    Werewolves : the occult truth / Konstantinos.
        p.   cm.
    Includes bibliographical references and index.
    ISBN 978-0-7387-2160-6
    1. Werewolves. I. Title.
    GR830.W4K66 2010
    398.24'54—dc22
                        2010022526

Llewellyn Worldwide Ltd. does not participate in, endorse, or have any authority or responsibility concerning private business transactions between our authors and the public.
    All mail addressed to the author is forwarded, but the publisher cannot, unless specifically instructed by the author, give out an address or phone number.
    Any Internet references contained in this work are current at publication time, but the publisher cannot guarantee that a specific location will continue to be maintained. Please refer to the publisher's website for links to authors' websites and other sources.

Some of the activities described in this book may be dangerous and/or illegal. Please exercise responsibility. Also, remember that what works for some may not work for you. As you proceed, use care, caution, and common sense. Llewellyn Worldwide Ltd. will not be held responsible for your personal actions taken in response to this book.

Llewellyn Publications
A Division of Llewellyn Worldwide Ltd.
2143 Wooddale Drive
Woodbury, MN 55125-2989
www.llewellyn.com

Printed in the United States of America

OTHER BOOKS BY KONSTANTINOS

CONTENTS

INTRODUCTION

Made of mud and wood, the hogan is a solid structure—the perfect place for Kiowa to hide. It is the strongest hut in the village, in fact, reserved for a person of honor. Kiowa's uncle. The shaman.

What would Uncle think of his little "sleeping wolf" cowering here in the dark while the rest of the village watches the rite by fire outside? Kiowa is ashamed, but cannot understand why he alone is afraid. He saw the villagers gather around Uncle earlier, and not one seemed to notice the sounds surrounding them this night. Did they not hear the howling? Do they not hear it getting closer now?

Only the sound of Uncle's chanting rises above the din. Kiowa can hear none of the villagers out there. Their silence may be due to sheer awe of the mysteries, or simply respect. None had asked Uncle what was so important when they came to the fire. It was habit for the village to gather when summoned, and to remain in attention as long as they were required.

Outside, Uncle's chant reaches a peak, and stops. The howling ceases.

Kiowa feels himself breathe for the first time in seconds. Another breath. A third.

Then something lands on the hogan's domed surface. Something big. The walls shake from the impact.

Kiowa falls against the wall, out of his crouch. He tries to listen, to understand what is happening above. A renewed burst of chanting erupts outside.

Kiowa waits. Softer pounding moves above him. The thing seems to be creeping up overhead to the center of the roof. Is it moving to the hogan's fire opening?

Faster chanting outside now. Should he try to run to Uncle and the crowd? Should he try to get away from the thing on the roof? To do so, he'd have to be able to move first, to overcome the electric fear that numbs his muscles.

Kiowa hears breathing coming from the fire opening. Heavy and raspy, the sound drowns out the chanting that is becoming even more frenzied. The breathing seems to not only come through the opening but to move around him, dragging across his skin like disturbed cobwebs.

A single, booming howl vibrates the hogan, and Kiowa starts to scream.

Little "sleeping wolf" wishes this were a dream.

A long, furry snout appears, and starts to make its way down through the opening above . . .

The preceding scene is a dramatization of a Navajo legend you may not be familiar with—a werewolf legend. It certainly doesn't sound like a scene from a typical werewolf movie or novel, does it? Actually, that unfamiliarity makes this legend typical in the world of werewolf folklore. Most of the legends from around the world surrounding werewolves or "man-wolves" bear little resemblance to the cinematic tortured souls who try to lock themselves in their rooms each full moon. Werewolves and other shapeshifters of folklore are as diverse as the cultures that believe in them. And these cultures are many; alleged true tales of werewolves seem to be almost everywhere.

Bringing us to what is perhaps the grand dichotomy of supernatural research:

Finding that a belief in something is shared around the world seems to imply it is true . . . yet finding contradictions in said belief's details makes it hard to accept the mystery at hand.

As we'll explore in the pages that follow, sometimes you need to look beyond the surface of legends to find potential commonalities. Rather than getting distracted by which nights a person can change into a wolf according to which people, we can look for possible hidden or "occult" truths that may explain why people from different lands have all come up with the same fantastic belief.

With that said, we can ask this book's core question: Are werewolves real?

Both the evidence you find in these pages and the conclusions you draw afterward may surprise you.

CHAPTER ONE

SEPARATING FACT FROM FICTION

Heed the words of the ancient gypsy saying:

Even a man who is pure in heart
And says his prayers by night
May become a wolf when the wolf-bane
* blooms*
And the autumn moon is bright.

This poetic verse was repeated by multiple characters in the 1941 movie *The Wolf Man*, and is easily the most memorable piece of dialogue in the film, if not in all werewolf cinema. Screenwriter Curt Siodmak didn't exactly have to comb through dozens of ancient manuscripts or inter-view surviving gypsy descendants to obtain this bit of verse, however. He simply made it up.

Most of what the average person knows about werewolves is a re-sult of Siodmak's efforts, right down to the idea that a human changes into a creature that looks a lot more like a hairy person than a wolf. That a film provides the classic werewolf for pop culture is not sur-prising—there is no furry equivalent of *Dracula* by Bram Stoker in the world of lycanthropy literature.[1] Okay, Count Dracula the char-acter was able to change into a wolf, among other forms, but that doesn't . . . count. Until recent years, novels had little to do with the popularity of werewolves.

Even though he didn't have a classic work of literary fiction to in-spire him, Siodmak should have done a little more digging into nonfic-tion or folklore. It turns out that the real werewolf legends are a lot richer than anything Hollywood has managed to capture.

APPEARANCE OF THE WEREWOLF

Werewolves of folklore were rarely described as looking anything like men or women with fur popping out of a neckline. Mostly, eye-witnesses reported seeing . . . well, wolves. It seems the very first ly-canthropy film—a lost, eighteen-minute short from 1913, *The Were-wolf*—had that right. According to reports, the film featured a Navajo woman who gets involved with mysticism and transforms fully into a wolf—a real wolf. Sadly, a fire in 1924 destroyed all existing copies, per-haps altering forever the future of werewolf cinema. Filmmakers who came after would avoid trying such a folkloric take on lycanthropy for several decades. Getting real wolves to behave on set was just too dif-ficult. CGI has made that a non-issue—as in the recent *Twilight* saga, with its pack of lycanthropes that change into enormous, but other-wise natural-looking, wolves.

Occasionally the lycanthropes of folklore were rather large wolves, too, as in the case of the Beast of Gévaudan, which probably should have been called the *Beasts* of Gévaudan. From 1764 to 1767, giant wolf creatures terrorized the French countryside from which they get their name. At least two of the beasts were killed and put on public display. We obviously have no photographs of these things, only crude drawings with questionable handling of perspective and scale; these artists didn't benefit from modern police-sketch training. Crude or not, the most famous drawing clearly shows a wolflike beast standing on all fours. Some eyewitnesses reported a beast that could walk either on all fours or upright, but most only made it sound like a standard wolf in stance if not size. Accounts from the era all seem to agree that these beasts seemed far too large to be ordinary wolves.

We'll have more to say on this case later on, but one other key point needs to be brought up here. No one witnessed a man turning into one of these beasts. Only toward the end of their reign of terror did the beasts start to generate more mysterious sightings, which bordered on hysteria. For instance, strange men with furry hands (but no reported wolf snouts) were spotted, trying to lure female travelers into the woods. Of course, for a region being plagued by wolf terror, it's not hard to imagine people seeing monsters everywhere.

For the most part, werewolf cases seemed very much like wolf-infestation cases. A skeptical reader would be justified in jumping in right about now and asking: Maybe they were nothing more than wolf infestations?

Despite their bad reputation in movies and fiction, wolves are not bloodthirsty monsters. They usually run in quasi-civilized packs that seem to coexist and act in harmony, as if they possessed an almost psychic group mind. A typical pack has complete respect for its alpha male or leader, and thereby does what the alpha feels the pack needs to do to survive. When a subordinate wolf becomes overly aggressive and goes against the pack, this is usually its way of announcing its challenge for the alpha position.[2] This could end up in a violent takedown of the aggressive wolf or a change in leadership. Most wolves, current and ancient, keep away from villages, and rarely sneak into children's rooms and carry them off into the night.

Still, it's hard to ignore the overwhelming lack of eyewitnesses in werewolf cases who actually reported seeing humans going through the throes of transformation. Rather than people claiming to see their neighbors turning into werewolves, it was the werewolves themselves who usually claimed to do the changing! You read that right. Unlike with vampires and ghosts, werewolves have testified on their own behalf, effectively against themselves, and have actually admitted being monsters in court.

Some of the accounts you'll read about went from being supernatural "cases" to actual courtroom cases. In a fashion common to all Inquisition "investigations," the accused would often confess their sins after a few rounds of torture, which would then lead to more rounds of agony. Once again, I can hear the skeptics, this time pointing out the obvious fact that people will confess to being the devil himself if the right number of hot iron brands are being pressed against their body. I say to those skeptics . . . read on, because I'm a skeptic, too.

Being a true skeptic means having an open mind. When I look over the oldest surviving records of "werewolf" testimony, I can't ignore a few peculiarities that stick out, especially when these accounts are considered in groups and not as isolated events.

SELF-PROCLAIMED WOLF MEN AND WOMEN

Three reasons come to mind why someone would admit in a court of law (even an insane, religious kangaroo court from the Middle Ages) that he or she was a werewolf:

First is the aforementioned torture. Ever burn yourself on a barbecue grill? Imagine that sensation repeated for hours. Again, no big surprise that torture will get an accused individual to "spill" words as fast as their blood can run to the stones below. Torture is likely the reason that hundreds of thousands of individuals, by most estimates, confessed to witchcraft. Think about those staggering numbers. Back in the Middle Ages, "witch" meant devil-worshiper by Inquisition standards, not someone who was a peaceful Pagan or herbalist. But even if you lump all mystics, sinister and sweet, into one category, hundreds of thousands of practitioners of mystical arts in the Dark Ages just seems like too high a number.

Second in our reasons why one might confess is a combination of confusion and mental deficiency. The Inquisition without a doubt manufactured or willingly accepted cases based on flimsy evidence. *Guilty until proven guilty* is probably a fair motto of this primitive "legal" system. An uneducated or even mentally deficient individual could get swept up in the pressure and drama of a court case, and basically agree with any wild theories suggested by the accusers. Even without torture. Tell a suggestive individual that he or she has sinned and has fallen prey to the devil, and that person may feel guilty and believe you, in hopes of salvation (which would come after a most painful end to life).

Third is the hardest reason to accept of all: that the confessors fully believed they could turn into wolves, even before they were caught and tried. As we'll see in one of the most famous werewolf courtroom cases, Jean Grenier was a young boy of about thirteen who went around bragging to villagers that he could turn into a wolf. His capture came soon afterward. He's not alone in such bragging. Other individuals you'll read about described the ritualistic methods they used to transform at will.

The first two reasons people would claim to be werewolves can't really add much to our exploration of a legend; they're both the result of coercion, after all. I'm not saying the reasons are not valid. On the contrary, I'm letting them go as givens—as explanations I fully accept. People were definitely forced or tricked into claiming they were werewolves . . . in *some* cases.

What about the times when there was no torture before a confession, and the individuals were not swept up in a court drama before letting out their first admissions? Confessors fully believing they are werewolves before their capture just makes for too intriguing a situation to pass up in our study of werewolves. The two coercion-type reasons for confessing seem to explain false positives in werewolf cases—the third category of true believer seems to point to something that could explain a whole lot more. If you'll pardon the expression, the cases of these self-proclaimed werewolves are the only ones that could add some interesting meat to our examination of human-into-wolf meat eaters.

Could it be that they were crazy? As we'll touch on, the once-supernatural term *lycanthropy*, which described a literal transformation of a human into a wolf, has fallen into use by psychologists as *clinical lycanthropy*, or the belief that a person can turn into a wolf. Clinical lycanthropy is a mental condition psychologists don't claim to fully understand. Medical case histories of lycanthropy are fascinating to read through, describing people even in present-day times who swear they turn into wolves, often in padded cells while white-clothed professionals observe otherwise. Delusion doesn't make for much of an occult study, but we have to keep it in mind when it seems the most likely explanation. Weeding out pseudo-phenomena is a must.

The most fascinating explanation is that these men and women didn't just *believe* they could turn into wolves. What if on some level of reality they actually could transform and carry out acts as wolves?

Reality is a tricky concept. I started out in college as a physics major at Polytechnic University, and learned quickly that the macrocosmic, tangible world around us does not behave in the same way as the microcosmic, quantum world. Some quantum phenomena resemble what has been called the paranormal. Not a topic you can merely touch on, this strange and wonderful fusion of physics and the occult is going to be the subject of an entire book of mine. For now, suffice it to say that science and the paranormal both are in absolute agreement on a few principles. One of these is the idea that what you can see and touch is *not* all there is to our universe. An expanded concept of physical reality may account for at least one type of werewolf.

Speaking of types, all is not equal in the realms of furry folklore. As I did in my previous book *Vampires: The Occult Truth*, I'll be classifying a supernatural being here into four discrete categories. Notwithstanding our inability to get a giant, salivating lycanthrope into a laboratory, we can gather data that ensure our categories are not haphazard groupings. It's true that much of the evidence in werewolf cases is old or even ancient, but that doesn't mean the data won't yield patterns when viewed en masse and compared. Having seen these similarities and causalities start to emerge from the mists of time, I added to them by analyzing modern evidence, experiences, and beliefs. To me, it all clicked. The combination of evidence old and new further solidified the categories given in this book.

THE FOUR TYPES OF WEREWOLVES

As you read about the four types of werewolves here and in the chapters devoted to them, please note that I will not be trying to convince you of their reality. I'm confident that they are organized in logical groups, and I will present evidence and occult theories that may explain them, but it will be up to you to decide if you believe in all, some, or none of the werewolf types.

Remember, it's possible to classify practically anything. You can organize the types of threats you'll face in a fantasy video game, for instance. Just because I can gather circumstances and evidence that mesh together to create these four types doesn't necessarily mean the types describe reality. The supporting evidence for each category of creature is the best I could find using available information and comparisons to other, more accepted scientific and occult principles. I don't necessarily believe in all of these classifiable types, but it will be apparent as you read which ones I may be leaning toward.

Involuntary Werewolves

No matter how "cool" modern movies may make lycanthropy seem, most people, if asked, would probably not want to join the furry ranks if they had a choice. The numbers of those against the idea of transformation would have been even higher during the Middle Ages. Back then, fear for the welfare of one's mortal soul ranked as high as fear for one's physical welfare. With piety, forced or voluntary, at an all-time high, it is not surprising that one of the types of werewolves from folklore is involuntary.

In films, humans were usually turned into werewolves by surviving the bite of a werewolf.[3] While a similar principle is found in vampire legends, this concept is found nowhere in traditional lycanthropic beliefs from around the world.

In folklore, involuntary werewolves were created as a result of someone being cursed or by being born under specific circumstances, which varied by culture. There's even an ancient Greek myth in which a god curses a man, causing him to transform into a wolf (this legend is actually where the word *lycanthropy* comes from, as we'll see). To fully examine this type of werewolf, we'll look at the power of curses and try to identify if it was possible to force someone into lycanthropy, real or perceived.

Voluntary Werewolves

More than a few fans of modern werewolf fiction would like to become lycanthropes themselves, despite how painful so many films make it look. What about people living in the Dark Ages? Despite the then-common fear of putting one's soul in jeopardy, some of our more ancient ancestors would still have welcomed the idea of becoming a werewolf. Not because any fiction of the day made it look "cool," though. The appeal was more primal, as power always holds allure for some.

Modern readers may be surprised to learn that, according to folklore, achieving transformation at will was possible if you knew the right rituals. We'll examine some famous cases of people who admitted to having used such ritualistic means to change into wolf form. Also, I'll be giving what I believe to be the first-ever occult analysis of the transformation rituals themselves and what their structure may indicate.

These rituals allowed control over when a person changed into a wolf. Unstoppable transformations at the full moon were not prevalent in folklore, being instead another trapping of films.

Otherdimensional Beings

While not technically werewolves or people who turn into wolves, phantomlike wolf beings have been sighted around the world. The evidence for their existence bleeds right into the modern day. Because of their seemingly etheric and not physical nature, these beings deserve mention here and not in a book on cryptozoology. The latter discipline looks for everything from dinosaurs that escaped extinction to Bigfoot, as long as these things are tangible.

Also in this category are wolflike beings that appear to shamans or other individuals while these people are in a trance state. Startling anthropological research proves that people in ancient cultures consistently came into contact with animal-like beings, including wolf men and women, when in drug-induced religious vision quests. Modern experiments with similar substances have resulted in virtually identical results, even if the participants had zero knowledge of anthropology. What are these animal-human hybrids that not only appear but also communicate with practitioners in altered states? Can they explain the origins of the belief in humans taking on animal forms?

Astral Werewolves

Strong evidence supports the idea that people who think they've turned into werewolves didn't do so here on the physical plane. As we'll see, some of the ritualistic methods that were supposed to help one achieve transformation contained strong psychotropic ingredients. Did these create hallucinations, or did they aid in a real out-of-body (and into a different kind of body) experience?

And what about rituals that created strong psychodramatic change in participants without the use of substances? Was it and is it still possible to work oneself into a frenzied state where a very real separation of consciousness into another form can occur?

Parapsychology literature has long collected accounts of people encountering living phantoms of friends and family members who were actually asleep elsewhere and possibly out of body. If this is really possible, what would these eyewitnesses see if the person astrally projecting was doing so in a wolf form?

With werewolves, fact truly may be weirder than fiction.

CHAPTER TWO

WEREWOLF BELIEFS
FROM AROUND
THE WORLD

Recall the dichotomy I mentioned in the introduction? When a belief is widespread, it makes sense sometimes to overlook differences between each of the cultures that share it and focus on why so many people believe in it at all. When a widespread belief evolves independently in cultures that had no way of communicating with each other, the belief is of particular interest—especially if the belief thrives for millennia in these multiple, isolated locales. Before it was possible to "spread the word," a word for something akin to a werewolf appeared for some reason on most inhabited continents.

A popular misconception is that all occult or paranormal beliefs date back to ancient times. Certainly the general belief in an unseen world is ancient, but a vast number of mystical beliefs and practices have either evolved greatly in recent years or have been newly developed within the last few centuries.

Ouija boards are a great example of a pseudo-ancient belief. While simple automatic devices had existed for centuries, spirit boards, also known as talking boards, were, despite romantic notions to the contrary, only developed in the late 1800s. Ritual magic, as structured by well-known orders such as the Golden Dawn, was greatly changed in just the last century and a half to the extent that it doesn't resemble what may have been practiced in early cultures. We can go on with examples, ranging from other Spiritualist methods for afterlife communication to the fact that Wicca is anything but "the Old Religion" (it likely dates to the mid-1900s). These examples all have roots in old beliefs, but are in fact modern inventions or radical reworkings of the old.

Not so with werewolves.

The belief in animal-human hybrids seems to predate true recorded history, dating back to actual cave-painting times. In later chapters I'll have a lot to say about this and how it may have led to the first beliefs in human-to-animal transformation. For now, let's turn our attention to the start of recorded civilization, where the first true tales of humans transforming into wolves and other animals were, well, recorded. Following these most ancient of tales, we'll move around the globe on a tour of where transformation beliefs flourished independently.

MESOPOTAMIA

Longtime readers of mine, those who have joined me on these occult journeys of exposition before, will have noticed by now that we
always seem to end up back in Sumer and other Mesopotamian civi-
lizations. No accident, this. The cradle of civilization—the land between the Tigris and Euphrates rivers, and part of what is modern-day
Iraq—is where written history literally began. Writing, on clay tablets,
was born here, along with the world's first advances in mathematics,
law, irrigation, astronomy, structured mystical systems, and literature.
Note the last achievement is not really the same one as the development of writing. Rather than just invent the ability to scratch shopping
lists into clay, the Sumerians were responsible for the first written he-
roic tales and religious mythology. And, evidently, the Sumerians created the first written werewolf accounts.

Written around four thousand years ago, *The Epic of Gilgamesh* tells
the story of King Gilgamesh and his dealings with gods and goddesses,
battles with monsters, and use of rituals to coax prophetic dreams.
Oh, and there is the minor goal of achieving immortality—epic stuff
from this first epic tale. Gilgamesh is not alone in his quest, however.
One of his opponents, the hairy beast man Enkidu, ends up becoming
his friend and fellow adventurer.

Enkidu is described in a colorful manner in the first tablet of the
epic, as these snippets show:

> *His whole body was shaggy with hair . . .*
> *His locks of hair grew luxuriant like grain . . .*
> *With gazelles he eats . . .*
> *With wild beasts he satisfies his need for water.*[1]

Okay, so this beast man at first glance seems more like a hairy hippie than a prototypical werewolf. His strength is prodigious, though, and he starts to terrify those who encounter him.

Predating the first incarnation of *Beauty and the Beast* by around 3,700 years, *The Epic of Gilgamesh* has the love of a woman cause Enkidu to abandon his beastly ways. It turns out that one of the wilderness trappers, frightened by Enkidu, asks wise King Gilgamesh for help. Gilgamesh sends the harlot Shamhat to seduce Enkidu. Her wiles have the desired effect. After a marathon seven nights of lovemaking (including the six daylight periods in between), Enkidu finds that the wild animals no longer approach or interact with him. His beast nature has been diminished. He eventually comes to the city of Uruk and becomes friends with Gilgamesh—a sort of Chewbacca to Gilgamesh's Han Solo. It is Enkidu's eventual death that leads Gilgamesh on his most supernatural quest, searching for the key to immortality.

If Enkidu was ever described as specifically dog- or wolflike, it was lost in one of the various broken tablet sections. That Enkidu is the first literary beast man is certain, however, making him another first for Sumer. Later in the epic, another wolf man is clearly identified as such, but he is mentioned only in an anecdote by Gilgamesh. The mention comes as Gilgamesh gives the goddess Ishtar a long list of reasons why he shouldn't be enamored by her wiles. One of the reasons portrays the idea of man into wolf clearly:

> *You loved the shepherd . . .*
> *Who was always heaping up the glowing ashes for you . . .*
> *But you hit him and turned him into a wolf,*
> *His own herd-boys hunt him down*
> *And his dogs tear at his haunches.*[2]

Did wolves have any supernatural significance to the Mesopotamians? The Maskim Xul, or Seven Evil Spirits, were widely known and feared in the area, blamed for many woes that befell people of the time. These evil beings were described in a chant that survives to this day. Of particular interest is the section where the Maskim Xul are listed one at a time, providing us with this line:

The fifth is a furious Wolf, who knoweth not to flee.[3]

Nothing else is said of the demon's wolf nature, but it's worth considering that one of the earliest recorded supernatural creatures had a wolf form. Later on, when we delve into the idea that some supernatural beings may have first appeared to humans in drug-induced visions, it will bear reiterating that wolf men and women were among the beings that appeared to many of our early ancestors.

Before we slip away from the deserts of the ancient Middle East, there's another tale related to werewolves we have to examine. This one hails from the great city of Babylon and appears in the Bible, of all sources!

In the third chapter of the Book of Daniel, King Nebuchadnezzar of Babylon builds a golden statue of a deity. He orders all who are near the statue to kneel and worship it whenever they hear the sound of trumpets, flutes, and other assorted instruments. Three Jewish businessmen of some type—Shadrach, Meshach, and Abednego—refuse to bow down before the statue when they hear the official music. This insolence enrages Nebuchadnezzar, and he orders the three men thrown into a fire. As the three predict, their true God saves them from the flames, even though the blaze consumed the guards who brought the Jewish prisoners to the furnace. This changes Nebuchadnezzar, and he accepts God as the true deity.

His religious awakening seems too little too late, however. In Daniel 4, the next chapter, Nebuchadnezzar has a disturbing and baffling dream that none of his astrologers and wise people could interpret. The supposed author of the book, Daniel, who was also known as

Belteshazzar, is the only one who can interpret the dream in the court. It's a troubling prophecy that the king will become a beast until seven seasons go by. This does come to pass in Daniel 4:33, with Nebuchadnezzar taking on the following form:

> . . . and he was driven from among men, and did eat grass like an ox, and his body was wet with the dew of heaven, till his hair grew like eagles' feathers and his nails like birds' claws.[4]

Thick hairs and claws? Sounds like quite a beast, and possibly a wolflike one. After Belteshazzar's prophesied, difficult-to-interpret time passes over him (Seven what? Days? Months? Years?), Nebuchadnezzar's reason and human form return to him.

Biblical scholars have found strong evidence suggesting that the Old Testament was heavily influenced by, and partially written and assembled during, the time that the Jews were in captivity in Babylon. This was hundreds of years after the alleged time of Moses (scholars have found no evidence to support his existence, and the first five books are believed to have been written by multiple authors). The tale of Nebuchadnezzar could be related either to something that the author of Daniel actually witnessed, or it could just be a wonderful catharsis. Nothing like getting a little literary revenge on the city that enslaved you by turning its leader into a monster.

ANCIENT GREECE

The first clear tale of lycanthropy comes from the country that originated the word *lycanthropy*, which is literally a combination of the Greek words for "wolf" and "man." What makes the story a little hard to believe is the convenient name of its main character, Lycaon, and the presence of the god Zeus in the story.

Before we delve into the tale, note that the ancient Greeks believed their gods to be among them all the time, in various forms and disguises. You never knew who was knocking at your door asking for food; that helpless old lady could be a vengeful goddess testing you! Yes, vengeful. Or jealous, or any human trait you can imagine. Along with the belief that deities were close to humans often came the belief that the gods were very humanlike as well, complete with both positive and negative human traits. Ticking off the gods was hazardous to one's well-being.

One of the gods' favorite pastimes or punishments was turning themselves or humans into animal forms. You've likely heard of Arachne, the legendary weaver who made the mistake of proclaiming her skill greater than the goddess Athena. When the goddess appeared to her disguised as an old woman, Arachne didn't recant her boastful ways. The goddess ended up turning her into a spider, the ultimate weaver, as a sort of ironic punishment.

The first werewolf, Lycaon, was guilty of much more than boasting. According to mythology, in the earliest days some humans chose not to worship Zeus and the gods of Mount Olympus. Some humans simply didn't care, while others thought their allegiance should really be to Prometheus, the Titan who had stolen fire and brought it to humanity. This fire is often interpreted to be wisdom, making Prometheus arguably the prototypical fallen angel in legend, similar to the later concept of Lucifer the light bearer.

Following a fallen Titan in ancient Greece was sort of like living in the Bible Belt today and publicly proclaiming that you love Lucifer. Those around you wouldn't be interested in hearing any deep mystical meaning you might have in mind. The locals wouldn't exactly kill you, but it would certainly make you a mistrusted individual.

According to one telling of the myth, Lycaon was just such an outsider who chose to follow the fallen ones. The difference is Lycaon had a little more clout than a typical villager would enjoy. As king of Arcadia, Lycaon had the mortal power to spout his views comfortably and to engage in inhumane activities that would further anger the gods. Zeus had learned of King Lycaon's views and great cruelty, and decided to pay him a visit in human form. In some tellings of the myth, it is only Lycaon's cruelty that warrants a visit from the king of the gods. Either way, recall that a visit from a god would not be an uncommon event for a character in Greek mythology.

The king received Zeus and invited him to dinner. Myths are often retold in different ways, so the motives behind what Lycaon did next are unclear. Some have written that Lycaon didn't believe that Zeus was who he claimed to be, and wanted to test the visitor's claim. Others telling the tale just point out that Lycaon was truly diabolical. Either way, what he did that night was not wise. Lycaon ordered the execution of one of the prisoners in his dungeon . . . and that the prisoner be made into a stew to be served to Zeus!

The god wasn't fooled and sensed immediately what was in his steaming bowl at the table that night. In a rage he destroyed the banquet table. Revealing himself to be a god, Zeus figuratively cursed Lycaon's cruelty and literally cursed the king for the rest of his days. Zeus turned Lycaon into a true eater of flesh: a wolf.

Was Lycaon's name just conveniently tacked on, or did his name lead to the use of *lycos* as the Greek word for wolf? Probably the former, as a god coming to dinner and turning a king into a wolf stretches even the most diehard occultist's faith in the unseen world. However, it's worth mentioning that Lycaon was not merely a fable warning ancient Greeks into pious lifestyles. For some, the mythic figure became a figure worth following.

The fabled king is the only werewolf to have an entire cult devoted to him and his interaction with the god Zeus. Ruins of the cult's meeting place still survive on Mount Lycaon in Arcadia, although details of the secret rituals that were practiced in this sanctuary are lost. A Greek geographer and explorer from the second century CE, Pausanias, reported that there were still human sacrifices being performed on the mountain while he was alive.

Keep in mind that the version of the Lycaon myth I have shared here is only one interpretation of why the king was involved with Zeus, but it is the one most closely related to lycanthropy. Over the years, having such a heritage in the area led to other werewolf-related beliefs. One is the idea that if a person becomes a werewolf, he or she can be cured by abstaining from eating humans for a set period of time (often nine years). According to Pliny the Elder, some type of lottery system in the area was used to select a man from Lycaon's descendants, the Antaeus clan, to be turned into a wolf. The selected man was brought to a lake in Arcadia and made to hang his clothing on the branch of an ash tree. After that he would swim across the lake and emerge as a wolf at the other side. If the werewolf didn't attack a human for nine years, he could then swim back across the lake and emerge as a human once again. If his clothes had managed to survive the nine years, I guess he could then put them back on.

Pausanias shared an interesting anecdote about one such Arcadian man who came back after nine years as a werewolf. Not leaving all his animal ferocity behind, the once-again-human Damarchus became an unbeatable boxer and won a gold medal in the Olympics sometime around 400 BCE. This story was old even during Pausanias's time, and makes one wonder what the basis for such a rumor could have been. The only kind of scandal you could have in sports pre-steroids? Whatever its origin, this colorful tale predates Michael J. Fox's uncanny prowess at sports (basketball in this case) in the 1985 movie *Teen Wolf*.

EUROPE INTO THE MIDDLE AGES

Putting much credibility into ancient epics and myths is difficult. The overused adage that there's truth to all myths makes it hard to imagine a god turning a man into a wolf at the dinner table. Even if it was based on some kind of real event, this myth would have been based on an event that was passed down orally for years before being written down. As with the New Testament of the Bible, which was also passed down orally for far too long before being recorded (and then subjected to poor translation), this type of passed-down history makes it impossible to guess what the original events inspiring the tales may have been.

The state of the art in recording history did eventually evolve, however. What do you think happened when lycanthropy legends started to appear in a time and place where recorded history had a way to actually be recorded and quickly shared? Enter Europe, after Gutenberg changed the world with his invention of the printing press and things get a whole lot weirder and, arguably, more reliable.

It is because of the printing press that a great number of werewolf legends from Europe have survived. The most notable of these will be used as the primary examples in the following chapters. For the purposes of this look at general regional beliefs, we will instead examine the more general forms werewolves were thought to take on in the various countries of Europe.

An important fact to note is that most areas of Europe lumped werewolves in with the belief in "witchcraft" or devil worship. This is not so unusual, considering that most of the continent was in the grips of religious mania and fear from the fifteenth to the nineteenth centuries, courtesy of that darling phase of historical irrationality: the Inquisition. They even had some well-respected literature to support their core philosophy—the claim that it was the devil creating werewolves, too. According to Saint Augustine, in his *City of God*:

> *But it is to be most firmly believed that Almighty God can do whatever He pleases, whether in punishing or favouring, and that the demons can accomplish nothing by their natural power (for their created being*

is itself angelic, although made malign by their own fault), except what He may permit . . . [5]

Augustine then goes on to give some wonderfully insightful ideas about astral werewolves—insights we'll examine much later on. But taken to mean any type of transformation, such religious writings didn't hurt the popular belief among the pious that God and the devil's cosmic chess match for human souls could involve shapeshifting. As far as the Europeans of the Middle Ages were concerned, witches worshiped the devil, and the devil allowed witches to turn into werewolves and other creatures.

Old English seems to be the origin of the word *werewolf*, which contains the root word *wer*, or "man." This "man wolf," however, was not a particularly commonplace belief in England. The seeming epicenter of lycanthropy is just a short hop across the Channel. No region in Europe was more inundated with werewolf beliefs than France, the prowling grounds of the *loup-garou*.

So prevalent were the beasts in France that we have more complete surviving cases or legends from this region than from anywhere else. However, diversity abounds with case density here. Just being from the same region doesn't make all werewolves alike. Most were described as looking like real wolves, but how they came to be in this state is a key differentiator of this book's werewolf types. And the *how* does vary.

Loups-garous were cursed into being as often as they were voluntarily created. Loups-garous were as likely to be phantom beings as they were hallucinations in the mind of the all-too-human beast committing heinous acts. The vast majority of accounts all agree in one way, though: religious hysteria permeates the tales.

Considering the beasts' various types of legends, the best definition for the French word *loup-garou* is literally "werewolf" and can't be refined much more. Expect to see this word pop up numerous times in these pages when we discuss everything from famous werewolf cases to methods for killing the beasts.

Not surprisingly, the power of religious mania seemed to have affected the beliefs of other European countries as well. Well to the east we come upon the land more commonly thought of for vampires. Romanian *vârcolaci* are peculiar creatures in that they are not clearly defined as just werewolves. Some sources have them as more ghost-like creatures, some as vampiric. A more specific type of werewolf from the region is the *bitang*, which is believed to be the seventh son born out of wedlock—a type of cursed or involuntary werewolf.

The belief in werewolves was so common in Germany that the creatures permeated even popular fiction. Witness "Little Red Riding Hood," for example, as well as more obscure characters from the Brothers Grimm. A common folk belief was that pacts with the devil would result in lycanthropy. In Germany, most of these seem to focus on farmers and their wives, being true tales of the folk. And nice folk at that, since in most of these legends if a husband becomes a werewolf, despite all his savagery he always manages to protect his wife. Touching, really. Werewolves even maintained a hold over public imagination well into World War II; one of the secret groups within the Nazi SS was called *Werwolf*.

Wolves have special significance in Norwegian mythology. One of the trio of fiercest monsters in these tales is Fenris the wolf. As a result, it's not surprising that an animal already attributed to a supernatural being would mix into other legends of the land. Norse warriors believed that they could obtain the characteristics of animals in battle by wearing their skins. These warriors would most commonly select skins of bears for their frenzied battle preparations, and were called *berserkers*, as they wore the *serks*, or shirts, of a bear. The belief in wearing skins was probably derived from the Völsungasaga myths, in which heroes Sigmund and Sinfjötli wore cursed wolf skins that turned them into actual wolves. Such pelt-wearing humans who turned into wolves were known as *Úlfhednar* in the mythology. One of the ritualistic methods for turning into a werewolf that we'll examine in chapter 5 was not all that different from what the berserkers and Úlfhednar did, minus the rage and lust for impending battle.

Ireland's werewolf tales are in some ways the most bizarre, blending the monsters into the legends of the saints. Forget Saint Michael slaying a dragon in some mythical battle in the heavens. These saints tangoed with the furry side right in the green grass of Ireland. While Saint Patrick is most well-known for his metaphorical driving out the serpents from the countryside (serpents may have represented Pagans), there is also a legend that he turned Welsh king Vereticus into a wolf. Some versions of the legend may have mixed with another from the region, positing that Saint Patrick cursed an entire clan to turn into wolves every seven years as a punishment for their lack of faith. Still other versions of the tale claim that it was Saint Natalis who did this "holy" deed in Ireland. Be wary of Irish saints.

The idea of turning into a wolf for seven years is also found in Armenia, where werewolves are believed to be women who are punished for their sins for this period of time. The sentence is carried out by a spirit who appears to the women and forces them to wear a magical wolf skin. Soon after, the transformation begins, with the female monsters developing a hunger for their children and those of others. Apparently the best punishment for evil in this country is to condemn someone to more evil acts.

In Poland, people are turned into werewolves for fixed periods of time, too, sometimes for as long as three to seven years. Here, the turning is rarely voluntary. Witches in the country favor lycanthropy as a curse, so locals are careful which women they cross paths with. A lot of the folk tales have to do with wedding nights, suggesting that perhaps the groom at one time snubbed the witch, choosing another young lady as his bride. Some of these stories even have the witch turning the victims back into humans after a period of time, usually by putting a magical caul over the wolf. One time this is said to have been too short a caul, perhaps on purpose, and the groom ended up keeping his tail after the transformation back into a human.

Overall, Europe was rife with werewolf legends, and a great many did involve alleged physical transformations. One that directly points to astral werewolves hails from Livonia, a Baltic province. This Livonian werewolf believed that he and others of his kind could travel out of body and transform their etheric shapes into wolves to battle "witches" in the underworld. Testimony from one such werewolf warrior will be looked at closely in chapter 11.

OTHER LANDS, OTHER "WERE"S

Other regions developed shapeshifter legends that, despite having a different animal as their focus, have startling similarities to legends from geographically isolated areas. One of the most prevalent shapeshifting beliefs that didn't center on wolves was the Japanese belief in *henge*.

Female henge most often took the form of *kitsune*, or werefoxes. They are often described as appearing in a seductive form. Call it kink if you will, but sometimes the seductive form *is* the half-fox, half-female form. Gives new meaning to the outdated slang associated with the animal. Male henge, or *tanuki*, sometimes took forms of timid forest creatures like raccoons or badgers, but could even transform into inanimate objects. Between the female's seemingly mystical powers of seduction and the male's ability to create illusions, the henge were a little more talented, so to speak, than typical one-trick shapeshifters.

Another talented multiform shifter is the *layak* of Bali. Like the tanuki, the layak can also change into multiple forms, including inanimate objects. It can even turn into humans! The *hamrammr* of Iceland can choose multiple forms as well, although it selects the form of the last animal it has killed. This multiform power even became attributed to the French loup-garou after it "left" the mainland and ended up becoming a new legendary creature in Haiti. In the latter country, loups-garous are not just wolves and can turn into most anything, despite maintaining the name that actually means "werewolf" in French.

People in multiple South American countries believe in were-jaguars, likely because the actual animals are more prevalent than wolves. Each country in the region adds a little local color to the legend, including differing tips on how to spot them. For example, in Brazil they note that just as female jaguars have numerous nipples for feeding their young, a woman who is found to have more than two nipples may be a werejaguar. It was not safe to have extra nipples just about anywhere years ago, it seems; in Europe, finding an extra nipple would qualify as a witch's or devil's mark, and would lead to a speedy trial and inevitable execution.

Africa is another continent to put an interesting twist on shape-shifting lore. In Kenya we find the *ilimu*, which is a being that can take on the form of a human. The concept of animal-human hybrids in Africa is persistent. The gods of ancient Egypt are a great example, appearing as they did most often with human bodies and animal heads. Sometimes they were drawn or described as taking on the pure form of an animal, such as Horus turning into an actual hawk.

The link between gods and animal forms may have an origin in entheogens, or hallucinogenic drugs that are used in a religious context. We'll be examining those in great detail in chapter 10, where we'll look at the spiritual types of werewolves. We'll take a close look at North America and Native American culture toward the close of the book, too. These American legends, both ancient and more modern, have a lot to add to our understanding of shapeshifters from an occult point of view.

Time now to exit our surveying mode of analysis and zoom in on our first type of werewolf.

CHAPTER THREE

INVOLUNTARY
WEREWOLVES
OF LEGEND

Most films make lycanthropy look like quite a cursed existence. The transformations look painful each time; your loved ones often meet an untimely demise at your paws; and, well, those damned villagers ultimately hunt you down with silver bullets or whatever other method the story relies upon. Being thrust into such a life does sound like a curse, doesn't it? According to multiple cultures it was not just a figurative cursed lifestyle, either. Being a werewolf was the result of a very literal curse. And despite what some movies portray, this curse did not take the form of having a body part end up within a werewolf's jaws.

As we touched on earlier, the concept of becoming a werewolf through receiving a werewolf bite and surviving it came from early horror movies, which often blurred the lines between vampire and werewolf lore. This cross-pollination of elements between the two types of fang-bearers is not unique to film. In some Eastern European languages, the terms for *vampire* and *werewolf* are often used interchangeably, and various tales even featured the peculiar idea that a werewolf who dies comes back as a vampire!

But the notion of a werewolf turning a person into a werewolf by planting a nonlethal bite? Pure Hollywood, no matter which sources you check.

According to folklore, there were two ways to become a werewolf against your will: being born into the nightmare, or being cursed by a powerful magician of some sort. Either way, you'd end up an involuntary werewolf—this book's first type of werewolf.

BIRTHRIGHT

Werewolf lore can give a whole new meaning to being born to . . . well, to do whatever amazing thing you do. Unlike being a blistering guitar player or natural comedian, though, imagine being born to transform into a wolf. Not what the typical child would hope for, right? On the topic of children's hopes, werewolves are uncannily associated with the ultimate holiday for children.

Have a Howling Christmas

Being born on Christmas was considered a bad sign in seemingly isolated parts of Europe. It's not difficult to imagine why people from the Middle Ages might have had mixed feelings about the holiday. Christmas is a few days after the longest night of the year, and obviously a cold night at that. Wolves would have been extra hungry and on the hunt for food during these cold nights, and remote villagers would have felt trapped indoors during the majority of this approximate time of year. Hungry, howling wolves, combined with bitter winds outside, would take their toll on the sanity of those who had a fair share of superstition to begin with. A common Scandinavian belief, for instance, was that on this night werewolves would gather and steal liquor from villagers, and then engage in drunken revelry . . . now there's a type of werewolf most people can relate to!

The association between lycanthropy and Christmas also manifested in the idea that any child born on this mysterious holiday was destined to become a werewolf. The exact day of the holiday that counts in effecting this curse, Christmas Eve or Christmas Day, varies by culture. Despite the startling idea that roughly one in 365 people would have been werewolves if the belief were true, the idea did flourish. Guy Endore picked up on this interesting bit of folklore and used it in his novel *The Werewolf of Paris*. The most well-known folktale involving this belief, however, comes from the village of Sant'Angelo dei Lombardi, which is east of Naples in Italy.

It's unclear what year this legend was supposed to have occurred, but it likely began circulating in the sixteenth or seventeenth century. As Christmas Eve approached (it was the eve, not the twenty-fifth, that applied in this tale), the village watched with suspicion and fear as a young couple prepared for the birth of their child. Apparently, everyone in Sant'Angelo knew what it would mean if the little one arrived on Christmas Eve. He would be doomed to a life of hideous transformations, and they would be doomed to defending themselves against such a beast.

Sure enough, the little boy arrived on the very night everyone feared. Despite their fears, the villagers couldn't bring themselves to punish the little one or his parents. In time it seemed as if their good will toward the family was rewarded. The child was sweet and pleasant, and played nicely with the other children.

Most days and nights, that is. For each Christmas Eve, the little one would turn into a little wolf. And not a cuddly cub, either. He would snap at anyone who came near, including his parents.

While he was young and relatively weak, the lycanthrope was easy to contain as each Christmas Eve came around. Every year found him a little bigger and stronger in wolf form, however, and it became increasingly difficult to restrain him when the inevitable change came. The villagers eventually had to change tactics and began locking themselves and their animals in each Christmas, allowing the growing werewolf to venture off into the wilderness. He would return every Christmas morning in human form, fall asleep, and basically awaken as if he were any other child.

While growing up, the boy knew he was actually a werewolf, but also saw that the villagers accepted him. The acceptance ran deep, too, for when he reached his twenties, he was allowed to marry a local girl he had grown up with. They were happy together, and of course had to make special preparations for their first and every Christmas together. Rather than worrying about where to hide the presents, the couple worked out a system where she would lock herself in before his change, and wouldn't open the door until he knocked on the door with three distinct knocks. This simple code would mean he was human again, and ready for her to let him in. After each transformation, she would let him in and wash off the leaves and probably worse material from his gruesome night adventures.

After a few years, the couple's arrangement seemed foolproof, which, of course, meant the wife was destined to become a little too comfortable with the routine. She eventually made a mistake that cost her. No witnesses were there that night when she either didn't lock the door or opened it at a time when she just assumed hubby must have changed back into human form. When they found the naked man walking around, still covered in the night's gore, the villagers knew his wife hadn't washed and cared for him as she had on other Christmas mornings. Taking him home, the villagers found the horribly mangled remains of his wife.

Surprisingly, the folktale doesn't end with the villagers punishing the werewolf. Instead his own guilt did him in, and the man soon after committed suicide.

Merry Christmas.

Lunar Influence

You wouldn't be much of a horror fan if you didn't immediately connect werewolf transformations to the full moon. As we've seen so far, the moon is not necessarily mentioned in most tales of animal-human transformation, but it does play a prominent role in folk magic and superstition, and therefore has seeped into werewolf lore. Oh, and wolves have really been known to howl at the moon. Or at least they appear to. Would it be splitting hairs (fur?) to say that wolves likely lift their necks for optimal airflow when howling, and as a result only seem to be howling *at* the moon?

Imagine the scene, though. You're a superstitious villager, afraid you'll never make it home despite the full moon's light reflecting off the snow and guiding you through the woods. Then you come across a wolf howling in that iconic pose. You wonder if it's merely a wolf or something supernatural, as everything looks more horrible when you're alone and vulnerable. Whatever this beast is, it has to be tied to the moon after an encounter like this, no?

The statistics involved in picking a single birthday that makes one a werewolf, such as Christmas, imply our world contains far too many hunters for the allotted human prey. Now imagine what the world would be like if being born or conceived on one of the thirteen full, or even new, moons in a year made one a werewolf!

For all the howling wolves on those nights, Europeans around four or five hundred years ago did not do too much howling in the throes of passion on the night of a full moon. A persistent belief was that if you conceived a child on the night of the full moon, he or she would be born into lycanthropy. In Sicily this idea was flopped somewhat, with the new moon or dark of the moon being the night during which you wouldn't want to conceive a child.

Conception wasn't the only thing to watch out for. Some people believed that being born on the full moon would do the trick. That's a whole lot of opportunities for a baby to become a werewolf!

The moon has a known effect on females, obviously, with some menstrual cycles aligning with lunar cycles. Why something so natural would be believed to also result in a malignant outcome is unclear. Childbirth was dangerous business in those days, though. Far too many children never saw their first sunset, let alone their first birthday, and mothers often died in childbirth as well. Superstition would commonly find its way into explaining things that had a taint of danger and that held a reminder of our mortality.

A common theme in werewolf lore is that whatever made you into a werewolf in the first place will also make you repeatedly transform from then onward. As with the Christmas Eve legend, a werewolf created by being conceived on the full moon would transform on the full moon throughout its life. Forget the astrology of what was going on with the planets at the moment you were born. All this almost makes you want to do a little reverse calculating to try and figure out what was going on in the heavens when you were conceived, doesn't it? Or maybe it really was a matter of being born on a full moon? Makes your furry forehead hurt; again, lots of opportunities to be damned with lunar-linked births.

Seventh Son of a Swinging One

Romanian folklore has a very interesting view of gigolos. While many cultures are particularly judgmental of females who engage in carnal pleasures out of wedlock, it's long been the double standard that such carousing is to be expected of men. We've all heard of sowing wild oats, sure, but sowing . . . werewolves?

According to the lands that brought us Dracula the ruler and, indirectly, the fictional king of vampires, even being a playboy can have supernatural consequences. The result of too much of this free love in Romania can be a *bitang,* or seventh son born out of wedlock.

Various cultures have occult beliefs surrounding the number seven and birth orders. In ancient times it was quite a significant number to contend with, being the number of known planets (again, in ancient times) and days of the week. Everything worked in a tidy astrological system with that number, and when it manifested in nature, you had to take notice. A seventh son of a seventh son could be a prophet, a healer, or a natural magician. It was just too amazing a manifestation to ignore in superstition, and it also influenced some famous fiction, such as Ralph Ellison's *Invisible Man* and even an Iron Maiden album.

Unlike the other beliefs associated with a werewolf's birthright, this one has an extra air of surprise. If you're born on Christmas Eve, for example, your parents "know" that you're doomed. If your single mom conceived you with a guy who then hit the road the next morning, you can't exactly be sure if you have any brothers and, more importantly, if you have six older ones.

As a result of this not knowing, versions of bitang folktales often center around a young man not realizing he is a werewolf until horrible events start being reported. He eventually uncovers the mystery around his upbringing, and runs off into the woods on all fours, perhaps joining a pack of similar illegitimate sons, who are legitimate threats to humans and livestock.

The seventh-son belief is not unique to Romania. In Latin America, particularly in Argentina and Brazil, seventh sons and seventh daughters were believed to become werewolves. Being a gigolo doesn't seem to have anything to do with it there, so at least the little ones could have the support of a large family as they expect their first transformations.

Argentina didn't exactly let the seventh-son belief die in modern times. At the start of the twentieth century, there was great paranoia and fear over the belief that families were actually abandoning seventh sons, giving them up for adoption, or, on occasion, even killing them. To quell this behavior, a law was passed in 1920 that made the president of Argentina the godfather of every seventh son born in the country, granting these children a gold medal at their baptisms and even a scholarship. The law seems to have worked, because they never took it off the books!

In Your Genes to Shred Your Jeans Monthly

Sometimes, folklore is wonderfully simple. What is one way that a werewolf can be made? Well, when a werewolf and a human, or perhaps two werewolves, love each other very much, they then . . .

It's not surprising to find that people in the Middle Ages would have thought you can inherit lycanthropy from your parents. The era is not exactly known for its advancements in genetics—okay, people from the time had zero understanding of how family traits are passed along. But basic family resemblances were understood, and the idea of looking like your parents or taking after them in some behavioral way was commonly accepted.

Inheriting the trait of lycanthropy had some superstition helping it along as a belief. Being a werewolf by birth is considered a form of family curse, and curses have been thought to pass on to children since biblical times and the concept of "sins of the fathers."

A recurring theme in the world of werewolves is to know your family tree if at all possible; there may be furry "branches" on it.

ACCIDENTAL WEREWOLVES

For every fleshed-out, prevalent legend in folklore, there are dozens of brief ones that have barely survived, and which have likely gotten mangled in the retelling. Tidbits abound in werewolf lore. The shorter, simple beliefs that follow represent some ways that could have been used by a person looking to become a werewolf, or could just as easily have been an accidental conversion waiting to happen.

You had to be careful what you ate in medieval Europe, and not just due to the lack of refrigeration. One of the most common beliefs was that eating the meat of an animal that was killed by a wolf would turn you into a werewolf. There were edicts made to ban eating such meat as a result, forming a royal precursor to the FDA. You also had to watch that your food wasn't infected with a peculiar substance that could lead to serious illness and hallucinations, as we'll see in chapter 8.

Eating random plants in the woods held a supernatural threat as well. In the Balkans there were varying accounts of a flower that, if eaten, would cause lycanthropy. Making matters worse was that the various versions of the legend totally disagreed about this flower's appearance. Was it the red, daisy-like flower? Maybe the yellow snapdragon? Or perhaps it was the white, sunflower-like plant with the sickly smell? Not that munching on any of them sounds particularly appetizing, but eating the wrong one was an accidental transformation waiting to happen, it seems.

Being thirsty while lost in the woods was just as dangerous. You couldn't just walk up to any small puddle and take a sip. That little puddle could be rainwater that gathered in a wolf's paw prints, and drinking it was another way to become a werewolf. Similarly, it was certain trouble to drink from the same stream as wolves, although no safe distance from their drinking is given and streams can be long. Some streams were even believed to be cursed, such as one in the Harz mountains of Germany, where drinking from the water caused one Countess Hilda van Breber to be transformed into a wolf. Her own husband had to hunt her down, although he didn't know it was her until after she was killed. Werewolf lore is full of such stories, in which a spouse only finds out after a wolf is killed that it was actually his or her mate.

While the mystical flower mentioned earlier seems tough to connect to anything historically or mystically, the idea that eating tainted meat or drinking water associated with a real wolf would transform you was a testament to the power of the belief in sympathetic magic. If the object you take into yourself is somehow connected to a real wolf, you run the risk of becoming a wolf as well.

The moon comes into play with conversions that could have been accidental or intentional. For example, some believed that merely sleeping outdoors under a full moon would do the trick. Other conversion legends involved getting naked and rolling around in the soil during a full moon. That may not sound at first glance like something you'd do by accident, but if you let your imagination go free, you may find that the latter was not so unlikely in a time without hotel rooms!

WITCHES, WIZARDS, AND GOOD OLD-FASHIONED CURSING

As we examined earlier, the first werewolf transformations of legend were caused by the gods. Mesopotamia and Greece both had examples of gods and goddesses—later on, the same is even true of the biblical God—getting angry at a human and turning him (always males in these cases) into a wolf. Ah, divine power and vengeance.

Humans trying to emulate divine power have always been the practical occultists of the world. Those who try to apply the occult to

change the world have been called magicians, witches, and sorcerers—
to give a few monikers. Such powerful practitioners of the arcane arts
were always feared, even if the worst they were guilty of was trying to
help farmers with weather or to heal villagers. Some earned the fear,
of course, performing decidedly more sinister rites. If you crossed
the nastiest of these evil magicians, they could allegedly cast a potent
curse on you. And in true emulation of divine legends and the powers
the gods were said to wield, this curse could involve transformation.

The practice of witches turning people into toads has become a
pop-culture mainstay. During the days of the Inquisition, it was no
joke. Through their alleged dealings with the devil, these witches of
folklore could travel through the air to be part of bizarre rituals held
in honor of, and supposedly by, the Dark Man himself. Their power
was such that they could cause any malady they wished to affect entire
villages. Turning a victim into a wolf would be relatively simple for
someone with such power.

This specific type of curse was the one of choice in Finland. In that
country, however, lycanthropy was not necessarily a lifelong curse. It
could sometimes be reversed . . . sort of. You see, if a werewolf was
cured by a magician, then he or she would often retain a wolf tail for
the rest of his or her human life!

As you might recall from the previous chapter, in Poland the predomi-
nant cause of lycanthropy is the curses of witches. As in Finland, there is a
tale in which a tail remains on the werewolf after transformation.

The French loups-garous were often believed to be those who were
unlucky enough to have crossed a witch. This belief survived when set-
tlers came to Louisiana, and resulted in the local *rougarou* legend. The
rougarou was supposed to be a humanoid creature with a wolf head,
and was said to haunt the swamp lands outside of New Orleans. Some
versions of the legend have the cursed person only remaining a werewolf for 101 days. Other versions try to tie the legend to disobeying the

rules of Lent. Ah, nothing like New Orleans for having wild activities around Lent.

It bears repeating that witches as portrayed in tales of lycanthropy are really just given that name as a convenient synonym for "servant of the devil." These servants would sometimes not necessarily curse someone, but instead they tricked people into becoming indentured servants of the devil, as in the legend of one poor shepherd in France . . .

Pierre Bourgot

During a terrible storm in 1502, Pierre Bourgot lost most of his flock of sheep and ventured out to find them and recover his means of livelihood. While searching, he came across three black horsemen. Note that the words *black*, or *dark*, always appear in descriptions of servants of the devil, but it's unclear if *black* is used in this case to describe the strange people's clothing, demeanor, supernatural features, skin tone, or all of these factors combined. These horsemen said they would help Bourgot find his flock and would give him money if he would swear allegiance to their master. Desperate, Bourgot agreed to these terms and to meet with them in a few days to fulfill his part of the agreement.

When they met again, Bourgot and his new acquaintances performed a sort of Black Mass, complete with the shepherd renouncing Christianity and swearing to stay away from the church. The leader of the dark servants, Moyset, kept the promise he and the others had made, too. Not only was the flock of sheep returned, but for as long as Bourgot stayed away from the church, his sheep were kept safe from harm. For a while, that one Black Mass resulted in happiness for the shepherd.

After two years, Bourgot tried to find his way back to his religion and attempted to enter a church. This return to faith was not to be, and he was quickly reminded of his dark promise by a servant of the devil named Michel Verdung. It is not clear if Verdung was one of the original three horsemen. He forced Bourgot to do a new ritual reaffirming his allegiance to the dark lord. During this ritual Verdung spread a salve of some sort onto Bourgot and onto himself. Bourgot was soon after horrified to find that he had turned into a wolf, along with his sinister "friend" Verdung.

Verdung and Bourgot went on to kill and feast upon children and adult villagers, allegedly in wolf form. They were caught in 1521 and corroborated each other's versions of this supernatural tale. After their executions, their tale was placed on the wall in the local church to warn villagers of the perils of leaving the flock, literally and figuratively.

Did Bourgot really join his new friend on these sinister adventures in wolf form? What was the salve that was applied to him?

Hallucinogens may have played a role in transformations such as this one, and we'll revisit this topic further, including examples from the present day, in chapter 10. In the case of Bourgot, the drama of renouncing his religion and being "damned" according to the belief system he grew up in may have added extra suggestibility to the mix.

CURSES—POWER OF SUGGESTION?

It may not be a werewolf movie, but *Drag Me to Hell* instantly earned recognition as a modern horror classic. Good storytelling combined with impressive cinematography is appreciated in any genre, and in horror it's somewhat rare. Even horror devotees like yours truly have to admit that in this genre things can go wrong pretty quickly in a film. Among its many achievements, *Drag Me to Hell* manages to say something very interesting about curses. As real as the effects of a curse may look to the person experiencing them—and in the case of a movie, as real as they may look to the audience going along for the ride—these effects could all be in the victim's mind. Seriously, watch this movie if you haven't seen it, or watch it again if you have. No spoilers here, but I can say this: even the ending may be nothing other than the main character, Christine, attributing something supernatural to a slip and fall, and her boyfriend may be seeing nothing other than a natural threat, considering where Christine ends up in the film's last scene. It's a refreshing, clever film, standing out from traditional Hollywood curse movies that left no ambiguity. In *Thinner* and *The Ring,* for example, only supernatural causes are possible reasons for the protagonists' misery.

Sometimes, life does imitate film. When everyone tells a character she's imagining everything, she might be doing just that. Are most curses nothing other than power of suggestion? To use the *Drag Me to Hell* example one more time, we have to admit that anyone who has seen the film has a hard time forgetting the gypsy woman's hideous visage and the shocking actions she takes to plant her curse on Christine. An effective curse has to work as potent psychodrama for its victim to get the "bad news" on every level.

Can such dramatic "magic" be enough to transform flesh? I've never seen evidence to suggest this is possible. Strong power of belief has resulted in more subtle psychosomatic effects, though. The best example of this is stigmata. Extremely devout people actually pray for the wounds of Christ to appear on them. Sometimes, these wounds do manifest. What's most fascinating, however, is that the wounds appear according to where the person thinks the nails went into Jesus' body. If the crucifix on the wall has palm wounds, palm wounds appear. If the nails are shown on the wrist, then it's the wrist. But these are wounds—and not ears, fur, snout, and tail, with dozens of bone shifts.

We need look no further than the placebo effect to get an idea of how suggestion affects the body. Science has proven beyond a doubt that some patients get better when given sugar pills, if they are told the pills are experimental drugs. Not all effects of a placebo require weeks of clinical trials to witness, however. During World War II, an American anesthetist named Henry Beecher had to perform an operation without any morphine, as he had none left in his supplies. After injecting the patient with saline solution, he and his nurse were astounded to see the patient relax and endure his operation wide awake. Beecher went on to repeat these salt-water operations successfully many times when wartime supplies of morphine were low.[1]

What if those who thought they were cursed only felt strongly compelled to act the part of wild men and women of the woods? This seems much more likely. Strong belief and walking on all fours, combined with a little howling, can create a rather strong visual effect to stumble upon in the woods. Especially if the cursed person had medieval personal hygiene to begin with.

The belief in curses persists to this day. One of the most common perpetrators is the type of name-changing, pseudo-gypsy fortuneteller who moves from town to town. Visit one of these Madame Zoras or Zeenas and you're likely to be treated to a half hour of cold reading and generalized predictions, followed by a serious warning that you have been cursed and that this is where all the problems you've admitted to having are coming from. If a lady who looks like she's straight out of *Drag Me to Hell* tells you someone else has cursed you, and offers to lift the curse for a fee, the drama of her saying so may fill you with sleepless nights or worse if you don't do as she says.

CHAPTER FOUR

VOLUNTARY
WEREWOLVES
OF LEGEND

Some of the most startling cases of werewolf trials contain those who proudly
admitted to having mastered the black arts.
It was the devil or his minions who granted
them the power of transformation, or so
they claimed. Why would anyone admit
such a thing during a time when merely
being accused of magical practice meant
likely torture and death? Could all of these
prisoners have been tortured into confessing

such bizarre actions and tales? Could all the ones who weren't tortured have been, well, insane?

This chapter will look at some of the most famous cases of voluntary werewolves of legend—this book's second type of werewolf. We'll explore why some of these people may have believed it was possible to transform at will through rituals and magical items. Also, through an examination of related occult lore, we will spend a moment reconsidering what the word *transformation* really means.

INQUISITING MINDS WANTED TO KNOW

The same environment of fear and superstition that led to the Inquisition also strongly affected the belief structure of the people living at the time. In the Middle Ages, the devil was out in the woods every night, calling his servants to worship him and pay dark allegiance. A shadow moving across the moon was a witch on her way to answer the call. A glow from a fire had to be a bonfire at either a Sabbat or Black Mass; it couldn't just be a wanderer keeping warm by a campfire. Even pious men and women had to believe that their very souls were in danger from all this evil around them.

The superstitious fear was not helped by the Black Death of 1348–50. Its effects were staggering, wiping out half the population of Europe. Witnessing such unstoppable death, and living in terror while waiting to see if it will affect you and your family, couldn't have done much to calm superstitious fears of the unknown. Many people witnessed firsthand that praying to God might not be able to bring much protection from peril.

With superstitious fear a given and the rise of the Inquisition, *mania* is the only word that can describe the persecution that began against people suspected of doing the devil's handiwork. Tabulating just how out of hand the mania got is difficult to do, but some regional numbers are startling. From 1520 to 1630 in France alone, there were 30,000 cases[1] in the "court" system that dealt with werewolves and witchcraft.

FAMOUS CONFESSORS

We covered earlier how the courts and the Inquisition used various cruel means to coax confessions from their prisoners. However, when you read the tales shared by these individuals, including Bourgot's tale from the previous chapter, you might have noticed that there was an awful lot of color and details provided by these individuals. Despite being burned or otherwise mutilated, they were able to provide quite rich narratives. Of course, this could just be because the details were suggested by the torturers, or the prisoners had learned of occult details from lore of the day and shared it in hopes of a quicker death. No surviving blow-by-blow accounts let us know how these confessions were obtained.

Peter Stubbe

In 1589, almost seventy years after the executions of Pierre Bourgot and Michel Verdung, a trial in Germany featured one hell of an admission of guilt by one Peter Stubbe. It's not much of a stretch to say that Stubbe's self-proclaimed motives make his story the perfect example of a voluntary werewolf, complete with magical means and sinister motives.

Precursors to the tabloids, detailed pamphlets were often printed in the sixteenth century whenever a particularly juicy story appeared. Thanks to one of those darling pamphlets printed during his day, Stubbe's tale has survived in sensationalistic detail. For those who haven't seen one of the titles of these types of publications, here is one with its archaic spelling and excessive description:

A true Discourse declaring the damnable life and death of one Stubbe Peeter, a most wicked Sorcerer, who in the likenes of a Woolfe, committed many murders, continuing this diuelish practise 25. yeeres, killing and deuouring Men, Woomen, and Children.

Who for the same fact was taken and executed the 31. of October neer the Cittie of Collin in Germany.[2]

According to contemporary accounts, Stubbe was obsessed with magic from a young age. The implication is that he used the grimoires, or books of magic of the day, to learn how to evoke and communicate with demonic entities. Rather than merely communicate with them and use them for specific goals, as I suggest doing in my book *Summoning Spirits*, Stubbe decided he had one use only for his etheric friends. He wanted to be able to transform into a werewolf.

During his trial in 1589, he admitted to having summoned the devil using his rituals. When the Prince of Darkness came, he offered Stubbe a magical item that is perhaps the one most commonly associated with transformation rituals: a furry belt, or "wolf girdle," which is basically a small version of the wolf fur that northern warriors used to wear when they wanted to summon the powers of the wolf. These girdles appear in werewolf lore as often as do magical salves or potions.

Somehow, putting on this girdle provided by the devil would not only turn Stubbe into a vicious killer, but it would also allow him to turn back into a human at will by taking the girdle off. It's unclear if the girdle disappeared when Stubbe became a giant wolf, but even if it remained intact it's hard to imagine how a wolf would be able to remove it. This seems to indicate that maybe the transformation was all in his mind, but I digress.

Stubbe used his powers to transform and attack those who wronged him, as well as those whom he lusted after, regardless of age. Most of the victims were found mangled and basically unrecognizable.

As far as forensic science of the day could determine—the science of naked-eye observations by hunters and townspeople, that is—the victims were eaten by one or more wild animals. What else would not only kill but also eat the meat of the victims? The villagers tried to ease their terror by asking a question they didn't want to know the answer to.

Assuming that he didn't really transform into a wolf, Stubbe was a cannibal. The crimes Stubbe would ultimately commit also included incest, as he fathered a child with his own daughter. Add to that his predilection for attacking and killing small children, and his place as a monster of nightmare is assured in history.

Listing all of his victims doesn't prove anything supernatural about Stubbe, of course. Jeffrey Dahmer accomplished just about as many atrocities and never thought he was a lycanthrope. But there is one more peculiar, anecdotal piece of evidence that we have to address, besides Stubbe's courtroom confession to wanting and obtaining the power of transformation.

Stubbe was hunted down and caught specifically because eyewitnesses saw a wolf carrying what looked like a small body. When the hunters picked up on the trail of the beast and closed in, they claimed to have seen the wolf turn into Stubbe before their eyes. This is beyond rare in werewolf lore: the actual authorities in a case seeing a transformation. Of course, it's hard to know how suggestible the hunters were. Maybe they really were chasing a wolf and came around a corner to find Stubbe, who was in the proverbial wrong place at the wrong time. The instant appearance of the man might have played a trick on the hunter's minds, making them "see" him transform rather than appear around a corner.

After confessing, Stubbe was tortured in a way the most jaded of modern individuals would find gruesome. To people of that era, the extreme punishment likely seemed suited to his heinous crimes.

Stubbe was stretched on a wheel until his bones were broken, had his skin slowly torn off by pinchers in at least a dozen places, was decapitated, and then, for good measure, had his remains burned. Nothing like being sure the guy's really dead!

As in most cases involving a magical girdle or potion, this one ended with the item never being recovered by the authorities.

Gilles Garnier

Stubbe was not the only werewolf who took delight in hunting young children. In 1572, the town of Dole, France, had its own monster with such a predatory preference, too. As with Pierre Bourgot, Gilles Garnier used an ointment that he rubbed on his body to transform into a wolf at will. Giving yet another example of confessions that are too colorful to be explained by duress, the way that Stubbe admitted during his trial to getting this ointment is peculiar.

A newlywed, Garnier was hunting for food for himself and his wife and wasn't doing very well. Apparently some type of spirit appeared to him in the dark woods and offered him a better way to hunt from that night forward: a magic ointment that would make him the ultimate hunter. Garnier accepted the ointment, applied it, and switched from hunting small forest game to hunting small humans.

Remember, Garnier was hunting that night for food to share with his new wife. Being a loyal husband, he kept to that goal! That's right. Garnier brought meat from his fresh human kills home for "lovey." Gives a whole new meaning to the term *mystery meat*, doesn't it? I wonder if she knew what her daily dinner really was.

Called the "Hermit of Dole," Garnier was never reliably reported to appear in full wolf form. He may be an example of a wild man who went a little too wild. After confessing, he was of course executed and joined the ranks of werewolves that somehow couldn't save themselves at the last moment with their magical powers.

Jean Grenier

While Jean Grenier's last name shares some letters with Garnier's, the similarity ends there. Jean Grenier's case represents one of the first to mark the beginning of an age of reason, but more on that in a moment.

Grenier is probably the youngest werewolf in folklore. When captured in 1603, Jean Grenier was a boy of thirteen or fourteen (we're uncertain of his birthday). Unlike most werewolves of lore, Grenier proudly admitted to his heinous acts before being captured. Much in the way children of today would brag about getting a cell phone before others in their class, Grenier bragged about being able to turn into a wolf and attack children.

Corroborating the werewolf's confession was a thirteen-year-old girl named Marguerite Poirier. She claimed that on the night of the full moon, a creature that looked like a wolf viciously attacked her without any provocation. Using an iron-tipped rod or staff that she was for some reason carrying, Marguerite managed to strike the beast and keep it at bay before it could bite her. It ran off into the night.

It was Marguerite's aforementioned attack that Jean Grenier began to brag about to an eighteen-year-old girl he'd had his eye on for what seemed to be less bloodthirsty reasons. Grenier actually vowed to this Jeanne Gaboriaut that he would marry her one day (werewolves liked having some domestic normalcy it seems). She was less than impressed with Grenier, but when she commented on his disheveled appearance he explained that it was only because of the magical wolf skin he wore. He claimed that with it he could transform into a wolf at will, and went on to describe his recent attack on Marguerite. In a bizarre form of sweet-talking, he added that were it not for Marguerite's iron rod, he would have killed her as he had done three or four other small children.

This wasn't the best kind of claim for Grenier to have made. As it turned out, the district of Gascony had been on edge over a string of missing children. Some of these little ones had disappeared while out-side, and some were even carried away from their rooms at night. It wasn't long before Grenier was in custody.

Grenier freely confessed to his crimes, and to desiring the taste of children's flesh, which he said was the most tender and plump. He told the court that after running away from his day-laborer father, who regularly beat him, Grenier became friends with a boy named Pierre de la Tilhaire. Pierre led him into the forest one night. As you may have guessed, the boys met another folkloric "dark man," who marked them in a ritual and gave them each an unguent and a wolf skin so that they could transform into wolves whenever they desired. Inter-esting that Grenier claimed to have both of the magical implements; confessors usually settled on one or the other. Of course, if the liquid was a hallucinogen, the wolf fur would certainly enhance the inner illusion.

As mentioned earlier, this was a landmark case of sorts. The court did not ponder whether the unguent and wolf skin existed or had magical powers (or even hallucinogenic ones). Rather, the court took pity on what it saw to be a sick or insane boy who'd had a rough start in life. Despite Grenier's proven murders, the court sentenced him to confinement in a monastery for the rest of his life. Any attempt at es-cape would result in execution. Grenier's friend Pierre de la Tilhaire managed to avoid capture, and it is unclear if this boy actually com-mitted any werewolf crimes, or if he was wrongly accused by Grenier for some other motive.

As a result of this merciful ruling, Grenier, who didn't try to escape, was not put to death. His remaining alive allowed for a rare follow-up visit to the werewolf in this case. Seven years later, in 1610, a written account was left by one Pierre de Lancre, who had visited Grenier at the monastery. De Lancre found Grenier to be gaunt and overall in a wild state. Grenier still liked talking about wolves, and acted like one several times during the visit, agilely springing about the room on all fours. He died in captivity soon after de Lancre's visit, never really providing an alternative explanation for his heinous crimes.

OCCULT TRANSFORMATION

Later, in chapter 8, we'll examine how a form of accidental poisoning that causes hallucinations could have accounted for much of what werewolves and even "witches" confessed to having experienced. For now, it's important to examine a different, more occult explanation for why some people sought out rituals to accomplish these antiheroic adventures.

The ancient grimoires are full of some pretty exotic promises. For those who haven't perused one, a grimoire is a medieval book of magical techniques. While a grimoire can contain anything from talismans to simple chants to herbal potions, the term is most often associated with a book of magic that contains rituals for calling forth entities. These beings are often of a demonic type, but there are grimoires that focus on everything from angels to elemental beings to intelligences that don't seem to fit into any categories, real or imagined. To those not accustomed to reading grimoires, the rituals found within seem exotic enough on their own, with their alien words and flashy accoutrements such as magical weapons. The descriptions of some of the demons and entities that you can call forth, however, are where things get truly surreal.

Oh, the promises! A typical grimoire like *The Goetia* has demonic beings in it that are willing to grant you riches, success, supernatural abilities, and, of course, all the voluptuous women you can ask for (most grimoires assumed a male magician, but I'm sure the demons would fetch handsome guys just as readily). And it wasn't just entities that could bestow these goodies on humans. Some folk magic, involving herbs and chants and no bogeymen, also promised mystical boons that seemed just beyond the possibilities of physical reality. How could a potion make someone love you? How could burning something make you invisible?

Medieval foolishness, for sure. No one in the last couple of centuries would expect magic could accomplish these outlandish promises. Or did they? As it turns out, very sane, accomplished men and women about a hundred years ago still crafted and practiced rituals designed to grant the magician, say, invisibility. Take a good look at the Golden Dawn's ambitious rituals sometime, and then read the roster of its well-known members. I know I still can't read an Algernon Blackwood short story without thinking about what kinds of experiences may have informed his seemingly fantastic plots and characters. For all we know, he really did have a chat with rambunctious, cloven-hooved Pan!

Invisibility is a good example to stick with for a moment, as it's a "power" that's promised throughout magical history. Did even the recent Golden Dawn members truly believe that ritually charging a cloak would allow it to make its wearer invisible? They sure did . . . if your definition of invisibility matches theirs.

You don't need to have light pass through you to be truly invisible, even though scientists are currently working on just such light-refracting cloaking devices. Think about what the word *invisibility* could mean. If you're ignored, you're invisible. If no one recalls seeing you, you weren't technically visible to them during that period of time. All experiences people have with magic in the modern day seem in agreement on this idea: magic is a way for your mind to create subtle changes in the physical world in accordance with physical laws. This holds true whether you light a candle and chant, or call forth a spirit to visible appearance (or to what you at least will experience as visible appearance—the jury's out on where the experience really happens, within your mind or without). Magic can only exist in our physical universe if it obeys said universe's physical laws.

Quantum mechanics has a lot to say on the subject, which is why my next book will focus heavily on how so-called magic is totally in line with what science understands to be true. Our minds really can affect the unseen world, setting off something analogous to domino-chain events that impact our macrocosmic, visible world. That magic can be real is mind-blowing for some, certainly, and the explanations are mind-challenging. But we'll keep the synapse damage to a minimum here and get back to invisibility and werewolves (magical theory will tie in, I promise).

Back to our example of invisibility now: say you've killed a chicken or knitted a silver sweater or whatever your invisibility ritual required. Chuckles aside, the most powerful rituals do have a strong dramatic or psychodramatic component—something that really tells your mind it's time to tune in to the subconscious part of itself that science has shown affects quantum experiments in controlled circumstances. One hopes you won't need to kill a chicken to get there, or struggle through knitting silver, actually, but whatever your ritual calls for should be exciting or even startling. What happens after all that psychodrama? If the magic ritual worked and you succeeded in activating a dormant part of your mind that can reach out and affect probabilities and other quantum phenomena, quite a lot will happen.

In time, that is.

At first you won't notice much at all after your ritual. But then you'll notice the primary person you're trying to avoid in your office will look the other way exactly when you show up late. Then, that annoying ex-boyfriend or ex-girlfriend will somehow get distracted when you walk by with your new beau, causing you to avoid another awkward social situation. And so on. If you really blasted that intent out there, the manifesting results around you could get even more obvious, complete with speeding past a cop who dropped something and looked away from his or her radar gun.

This isn't a book on magical practice, but you're free to experience the types of phenomena I just described by picking up one of my books on the subject, if dark aesthetics and the thought of dark psychodrama please you. Or you may want to dig up a book from another author if you think your psychodrama should be more of the cheery, rituals-performed-by-sunlight type.

Now, back to werewolves. When you read the ritual elements in the next chapter, you'll see how psychodramatic some of them really are and how effectively shocking they would have been to the superstitious folks performing them back in the day. Think back to the example of invisibility, and imagine what it might have been like to believe that those around you would perceive you as a wolf. The placebo effect we talked about with curses proves that magic may have the strongest effect in our own bodies. Combine the placebo effect with a person's questionable reasons for seeking ritual transformation into a wolf, and you could have a dangerous result.

It's hard to fathom a noble reason why most people would have sought out a ritual for becoming a werewolf; most motives would have been sinister. The case histories in this chapter bear that out, describing individuals who wanted to be able to hunt, kill, and usually eat human victims. They could have been suffering from medical lycanthropy, sure, but they could have just as likely been so filled with bloodlust that the supernatural means afforded them was too appealing to pass up. Much like Jeffrey Dahmer and other serial killers have used certain sexual social "scenes" to their advantage, voluntary werewolves who turned to magic may have just been using the "scene" available to them. Everyone believed in werewolves and magic, so why shouldn't these miscreants take advantage of the current craze?

Performing these rituals during the superstition-charged sixteenth and seventeenth centuries would have been a lot more effective than performing them today. Voluntary werewolves could have gotten effects combining psychosomatic phenomena, hallucinations, and magic that just made it all fall together for the inner "wolf" experiencing the whole event. There's nothing more powerful than Thanatos and Eros, our latent obsessions with death and sex. For some people, performing a ritual to become a werewolf was the ultimate way to tap into at least the death urge (possibly the sex urge, too, although nonexistent forensics of centuries past couldn't identify everything that was done to female victims). The rituals might not have generated a single patch of fur or extended a tooth or nail, but they would have certainly created a change.

With that said, think wisely before trying the ritual techniques in the next chapter!

CHAPTER FIVE

WEREWOLF RITUALS

Frequent readers of mine have come to expect my books to have either a mostly how-to angle, or at least some type of how-to chapter. While *Vampires: The Occult Truth* satisfied that requirement with techniques designed to keep away phantom visitors from your bedroom, this sister book takes a slightly different approach.

In the previous chapter we touched on how occultism has traditionally had slightly different interpretations of words such as *invisibility* or *transformation*. The grandiose promises of the grimoires were not always literal. Does this kind of interpretation apply to the magic said to have come from the werewolf-transformation techniques provided by the Dark Man of witches' Sabbats?

When you read the following ritual descriptions, suspend a little disbelief and pretend you're actually trying to find out how to turn yourself into a furry one next full moon. When read in this light (lunar light?), the rituals may inspire or evoke some of the psychodrama that the original practitioners felt long ago. Getting a sense of the possible terror or excitement they may have experienced will help you appreciate what the effects may have been on the original practitioners.

THE USE OF BOTH GIRDLE AND SALVE

The following ritual combined the use a wolf belt or girdle as well as a salve. One famous werewolf said to use both an applied substance and a skin of some type was Jean Grenier, although the following ritual has never been specifically attributed to him as one he originated or used. Who first recorded this ritual, thereby allowing it to survive into the present day, is unknown, but it eventually saw mass publication in Elliott O'Donnell's 1912 book, *Werwolves*. O'Donnell was an early-twentieth-century ghost hunter and the author of dozens of books.

Lest anyone doubt that psychodrama was a key ingredient in getting some kind of result from a werewolf rite, look at the type of admonition that usually accompanied such a ritual when it was written about in centuries past. The following example of such a precursor is taken from O'Donnell's book:

> *In the first place, it is necessary that the person desirous of acquiring the property of lycanthropy should be in earnest and a believer in those superphysical powers whose favour he is about to ask.*[1]

Besides the stilted language and the archaic spelling of the book's title, the message is evolved from an occult point of view. O'Donnell is reminding the reader to be open to the psychodrama before he or she ventures out into the night, bizarre ingredients in hand.

As for the ingredients you're about to encounter, please note that they contain substances known to cause everything from hallucinations to, well, more poisonous effects. This is an ancient ritual and not a cookbook for a yummy drink!

Also, there may be an element that is disturbing to some: the fat of a freshly killed animal. While the rite calls for the fat of a cat (I imagine for its symbolic and obvious anti-canine nature), ritual elements can almost always be substituted for things that make sense. In this case, a visit to a butcher would provide plenty of suitable fat, even though it obviously won't be from a cat, assuming you have a perfectly sane butcher in your neighborhood.

Then there's the slightly tricky matter of obtaining enough furry wolf skin for you to tie around your waist as a belt or girdle.

Even though this ritual is really being included for scholarly occult purposes, for providing a glance into another time, some of you may end up trying it in either exact or slightly modified form. So consider local controlled substance laws as well as animal cruelty laws if you do decide to try this in the modern day.

Note that even though this ritual was recorded in O'Donnell's book,[2] and the italicized chants are taken from that source, I have fleshed out the instructions for performing it for the benefit of modern readers.

By Girdle and Salve

Locate a remote spot in the true wilderness, well away from any villages or even remote residences. This "wilderness" can be deep in the woods, on a mountain top, or even in a desert. Total seclusion is critical to ensuring that the dark powers summoned will answer.

Visit the ritual area by daylight and choose the most level piece of ground. Depending on the likelihood of its being discovered, and the value of the contents, a cache of at least some of the ritual items you plan on using can be left in the area. I'd recommend only doing so if you're visiting on the same day you plan on performing the rite (during the new moon).

On the night of the new moon, spend a few moments reaffirming what it is you wish to accomplish this night. Then, venture out to your remote spot with whichever supplies mentioned in this section that you didn't leave behind earlier. It is okay if you were waiting or camping near the ritual area, but do not actually be in the ritual area as the sun sets. Only approach the spot well after dark to begin preparing for the rite. Preferably, you will be able to wait until about a half hour before midnight to enter the area, although this will vary based on how difficult the area is to reach.

Light an oil lamp to guide your way to the spot and to allow you to see as you make your preparations.

Create a physical circle on the flat area of ground using any means appropriate to the terrain. Draw in the dirt or sand with a stick, mark stone with chalk, or lay something out such as rope or rocks. Whatever method you use to create it, make sure this outer magic circle is at least fourteen feet in diameter.

Using the same method you used to create the first circle, create an inner circle that is six feet wide.

Within the inner circle, light a fire using kindling from the ritual area if possible.

Place some type of camp-cooking apparatus over the fire. This can be an iron tripod or some type of small iron grill cover.

Heat an iron vessel or pot of water on your small setup until it approaches a boil.

At exactly midnight, place into the boiling water approximately one handful each of any three of the following ingredients:

Asafoetida
Parsley
Opium
Hemlock
Henbane
Saffron
Aloe
Poppy seed
Solanum

Close your eyes for a few moments and breathe in the aroma coming from the boiling pot.

Open your eyes, peer out into the darkness, and recite the following words loudly and clearly into the night:

Spirits from the deep
Who never sleep,
Be kind to me.

Spirits from the grave
Without a soul to save,
Be kind to me.

Spirits of the trees
That grow upon the leas,
Be kind to me.

Spirits of the air,
Foul and black, not fair,
Be kind to me.

Water spirits hateful,
To ships and bathers fateful,
Be kind to me.

Spirits of earthbound dead
That glide with noiseless tread,
Be kind to me.

Spirits of heat and fire,
Destructive in your ire,
Be kind to me.

Spirits of cold and ice,
Patrons of crime and vice,
Be kind to me.

Wolves, vampires, satyrs, ghosts!
Elect of all the devilish hosts!
I pray you send hither,
Send hither, send hither,
The great gray shape that makes men shiver!

Shiver, shiver, shiver!
Come! Come! Come!

Allow any energy you feel to peak as you almost yell the last six words.

Immediately take off your shirt and apply a pre-made, fat-based salve to your skin. This should be a mixture that you prepared from the fat of a newly killed animal (see the opening notes to this rite). Blended into this fat base should be aniseed, camphor, and opium (see notes again!).

Pass a belt or girdle made of wolf skin over the steam from the boiling pot, allowing the steam to rise up around the wolf skin and meet your nose. Do the passing motion three times, then tie the girdle around your waist.

Kneel down before the boiling pot, continuing to smell the mixture. Peer into the darkness through the steam and let your vision blur slightly.

It is now time to wait for the "Unknown" to manifest itself. The fire may burn blue and suddenly die out, or some other sign may announce the presence of this Unknown. You may detect a deep unnatural silence, or the extreme opposite: the sounds of crashes and bangs, groans and shrieks. If you see nothing, you may only feel abnormal cold and a sense of dread. If you do see something approach, it could be the form of a simple huntsman or something more hideous, part man and part beast. The approaching form could be clearly defined, or misty and ethereal. Not much is known about this being's true nature, only what it is supposed to be able to grant to the man or woman who summons it.

When you detect its presence in some form, the change will begin . . .

How It May Work

In many ways, the preceding ritual is the ultimate werewolf rite. In addition to containing both a salve and a girdle, it contains another element that seems to come up repeatedly in folklore: the idea of a mysterious being encountered in the wilderness.

Called the "Unknown" in this rite, the entity is clearly supposed to be the thing that visibly or invisibly provides the final magic touch, if you will. In some of the folklore, the confessing werewolves would admit to accepting a girdle or salve from a dark man in the woods. This ritual may mix up the order a bit, implying that you have to supply the materials and then call the mysterious being forward to give them a dark blessing of sorts.

So, what is really happening here? First, we can't ignore the materials being used. Combining any three of the ingredients listed in the boiling pot is guaranteed to produce vapors that will affect one's consciousness. The ingredients are similar to those used in witch-flying ointments from the fifteenth to eighteenth centuries, and could send the ritual participant into quite a "flight" indeed. These ingredients have been known to kill as well, so this rite is not without unreasonable risk. At the very least, avoid drinking the boiling concoction.

Say the vapors begin to get the participant in an altered state, and he or she is fully invested in the ritual to begin with. This combination of hallucinogen and willpower or intention may be enough to get someone launched into a hyper-realistic "trip."

Now add the strange words of the rite. Vampires and ghosts are mentioned, perhaps to play on the primal fears of the participant. It's a wonderfully orchestrated piece of psychodramatic prose. Combined with the lonely setting, surely all this is enough to do something to the participant's subconsciousness.

Yet the rite goes on to add a salve, which may or may not absorb into the bloodstream to help along the drug-aided mood. And, of course, the physical symbol of the form desired comes onto the participant. The wolf skin is really a perfect final touch.

So, is the entire rite a perfect launching point for an imagined experience? Sort of like popping LSD in a room surrounded by *Star Wars* toys and ending up on the Death Star? It certainly could be.

But there is one more possibility. This ritual has most of the elements found in traditional magical evocation, or the practice of summoning a spirit to visible appearance. Even after having practiced numerous of those rituals myself and authoring a book on the subject, I still can't say that summoning spirits involves anything more than calling forth something that you alone can see and you alone can hear as if it is standing before you. The psychodrama in an evocation is so powerful that it works. Then, as if snowballing the effect, the psychodrama of the ritual having worked seems to fuel whatever it is you desire.

Magic never seems to violate natural laws, as we've covered. So I'm not of the opinion that the above ritual will really result in psychodrama-induced gooseflesh turning into wolf fur. However, the combination of the mind-altering substances and the ritual might be enough to make it real to the participant in every way that matters. Again, if the placebo effect can heal someone taking a sugar pill, magic like the preceding rite should be able to make changes just shy of Lon Chaney's *Wolf Man* in someone giving the rite his or her all.

When this ritual is performed, one of three things will happen in all likelihood:

The first is that the participant will pass out and have either a vivid hallucination of being a wolf, or not. The "not" could be because the participant was too strongly affected by the poison and may not ever awaken again.

Second is the possibility that the ritual will fire on all psychological cylinders, sending the participant howling into the woods. He or she will believe absolutely that anyone encountering him or her will see a wolf . . . and anyone encountered will absolutely agree that the participant is at least a "wild person" of the woods. If you saw someone wearing only tattered pants and a wolf skin, howling and filthy from moving through the brush, you would certainly let the dark play tricks on you. I'd imagine you'd run, hoping to survive to tell the tale (which will get better and more Lon Chaney-like with the retelling).

The third thing that could happen after such a rite is something we'll be examining in depth in chapter 11. The ritual may knock the practitioner unconscious, and may provide a seemingly hallucinated fantasy hunt in the woods. But what if everything the person saw in this dream actually came to pass, being perpetrated by what others would see as a glowing, astral wolf?

ALTERNATIVE CHANTS AND INGREDIENTS

Even though the girdle-and-salve rite literally has it all, I want to include a couple of other chants and their associated ritual elements found in the existing werewolf lore. Because the actual words used in a ritual are mostly for psychodrama, you can mix and match these elements at liberty the next time you feel the overwhelming need to get a little furry by night.

The old grimoires always used to provide additional chants in case a spirit failed to appear. This wasn't because the entity didn't like your choice of words, but more likely to provide further ways to deepen the psychodramatic reaction and trance of the practitioner. The following chants have been used either in tandem with the previous rite or as replacements for what is said after the pot of hallucinogenic stew is boiling.

The Unknown Once Again

The first chant also refers to the thing from the woods as the "Unknown":

Come, spirit so powerful! Come, spirit so dread.
From the home of the werewolf, the home of the dead.
Come, give me thy blessing! Come, lend me thine ear!

Oh spirit of darkness! Oh spirit so drear!
Come, mighty phantom! Come, great Unknown!
Come from thy dwelling so gloomy and lone.
Come, I beseech thee; depart from thy lair.
And body and soul shall be thine, I declare.

Haste, haste, haste, horrid spirit, haste!
Speed, speed, speed, scaring spirit, speed!
Fast, fast, fast, fateful spirit, fast![3]

The practitioner is then supposed to strike his or her head three times on the ground instead of applying a salve or wearing a wolf skin. Perhaps this is an even more effective method of reaching an altered state of awareness? Or at least it's a way to lose consciousness if the chosen ritual area happens to be particularly rocky!

Kiss the Ground

The following short chant contains some pretty strong statements, but is oddly often followed by a more gentle way to meet the ground with one's head:

Make me a werewolf! Make me a man-eater!
Make me a werewolf! Make me a woman-eater!
Make me a werewolf! Make me a child-eater!

I pine for blood! Human blood!
Give it to me! Give it to me tonight!
Great Wolf Spirit! Give it to me, and heart, body, and soul, I am yours![4]

At this point, the practitioner gently kisses the ground three times and awaits the spirit from the woods.

What's peculiar about the above rite, besides the fact that such a short chant and simple act could turn someone into a werewolf, is that this type of Earth reverence by kisses would be used for a more grounding effect in a typical ritual. Grounding is literally when people expel extra energy in a ritual by directing it down. Kisses are seldom used, but they would work in this role. It's bizarre that such a calming action like kissing the ground would be relied upon as a peak moment in this ritual.

From Russia with Fur

The following charming charm comes from Russia, where apparently very little ritual activity is required to effect a transformation into a lycanthrope. One silly warning before we proceed, though. According to legend, Russian werewolves have a barbed tongue in human form, so think wisely before choosing to become this type of lycanthrope as you will be instantly recognizable by day.

A note on the spell itself: I can't find a Russian version of the words used in the ritual, and therefore can't vouch for whether the chant itself was added later to complement the simple actions described.

The rite begins with venturing into the forest and finding a chopped-down aspen tree, or one that was hit by lightning, or perhaps one you just cut down for the purpose of this ritual.

Take a copper knife and stab the stump. Then, walk around the tree, saying the following:

In the wide sweeping ocean, on the island of Bujan
On the open plain the moon shines on an aspen stump
Into the green wood, into the gloomy veil.

Towards the herd creeps a shaggy wolf
His fangs sharpened for the horned cattle

But into the woods the wolf does not go
He dives not into the shadowy vale
Moon, moon!

Golden horned moon!

Melt the bullet; blunt the hunter's knife
Splinter the shepherd's staff
Cast terror upon all cattle
Upon men and all creeping things
That they may not seize the gray wolf
That they may not rend his warm hide!

My word is binding, firmer than sleep
More binding than the promise of heroes![5]

After the last line, jump over the tree three times to complete the rite.

When you're done with your night of prowling, I assume you can come back and remove the knife to turn into a human. Good luck with that lack of opposable thumbs.

Yet Another Exotic Recipe

It's not possible to provide enough warnings against the use or ingestion of bizarre mixes from the grimoires. Still, I feel it would be of interest to many to see another authentic recipe for a werewolf-transformation ointment. (And, honestly, it will only help drive the point home later on, when we discuss the role of hallucinations in the transformation process.)

The following is a recipe from the 1615 treatise *De la Lycanthropie, Transformation et Extase des Sorciers*, by Jean de Nynauld:[6]

Belladonna root

Nightshade

The blood of bats and hoopoes

Aconite

Celery

Soporific nightshade

Soot

Cinquefoil

Calamus

Parsley

Poplar leaves

Opium

Henbane

Hemlock

Varieties of poppy

Crustaceans

Hard to beat that for completeness!

Note that in another old treatise, Giovanni Della Porta's *Natural Magic* (1658), we are warned about what such ingredients may do to the user. While the descriptions are not wolf-related, they clearly illustrate an imagined feeling of animal shapeshifting:

> *By drinking [the] potion, the man would seem sometimes to be changed into a fish; and flinging out his arms, would swim on the ground: sometimes he would seem to skip up, and then dive down again. Another would believe himself turned into a goose, and would eat grass, and beat the ground with his teeth . . . this he did with [mandrake, deadly nightshade, and henbane].[7]*

Again, consider passing on such mixtures.

The techniques you've just read about range in complexity and level of danger involved. If you'd like to try a type of werewolf change, but you're not up to all the extensive ritual requirements, you may find what you're looking for in chapter 11. Odd as it may sound, you'll read about a technique that allegedly works, and only involves staring at six black lines.

CHAPTER SIX

KILLING
AND CURING
WEREWOLVES

Poor werewolves—whether in film or folklore, it always ends poorly for them. No tale of lycanthropy is complete without the inevitable death of its starring monster or dark antihero. In film, it's usually a silver bullet that does the deed, accompanied by a dramatic return of the monster to human form just before or after death. In folklore, it's most often the torturers of the Inquisition that do the creatures in; surprisingly, none of the imprisoned werewolves ever transform and fight back.

This chapter is a would-be werewolf hunter's guide of sorts, with both violent and were-humanitarian options (yes, lycanthropy did have some cures) provided for when you find the beasty. As many methods for killing and curing the beings exist as there are cultures that believe in werewolves. We'll avoid any duplication, and group them together here for simplicity, giving historical information where relevant. For example, the origin of the belief in silver's lethal nature may be of particular interest to occult purists and even horror movie fans.

With that said, if you happen to be so inclined, happy hunting!

SILVER BULLETS, SILVER CANES, SILVER . . . YOU GET THE IDEA

In the realm of vampire movies, the most well-known way to kill the undead is by exposing the creature to sunlight. With a few exceptions, this is an element people expect to see in their fiction. And it is fiction! F. W. Murnau killed off his vampire in the 1922 film *Nosferatu* via sunlight in an attempt to avoid being sued by the Bram Stoker estate for completely lifting the *Dracula* storyline. While the trick didn't work, and *Nosferatu* the film was itself ordered destroyed (fortunately a copy did survive), the sunlight idea caught on in pop culture and fiction. In most folklore, vampires can hunt by day or night if they really wish to, but the average person still doesn't know that.

Here's where you're expecting me to provide a similar story behind silver bullets and other silver weapons. The use of a substance like that has to be a screenwriter's invention, right? Silver killing something that hunts by moonlight just sounds too Hollywood.

Nope. As made-for-film as it sounds, the concept of a silver item being able to kill werewolves is straight out of folklore.

The first recorded instance of silver being the go-to weapon comes from 1640, and a werewolf epidemic that plagued the city of Greifswald. We have no way to account for the validity of these passed-down claims, but according to local legends the town was infested with the creatures. Werewolves were gradually outnumbering the humans and killing off the ones that remained. Granted, the tale was recorded about two hundred years afterward, but it is astounding that an event that allegedly affected so many people was passed on for centuries without being challenged by the locals. No one stepped forward to say that Grandpa wasn't really mauled by a wolf at all, for instance.

Assuming the 1640 event had at least some basis in fact, how was this plague dealt with? Surprisingly, by a group of students. They fought as best as they could and weren't doing so well, supposedly proving that these were no ordinary wolves. Then, one of them decided to try something for a reason that has been lost to legend. This student suggested melting down all the silver they could find to manufacture what he hoped would be lethal balls for their muskets. He must have been inspired, because his bullets were lethal to the wolves indeed. These little balls of silver supposedly killed off the entire werewolf population, both returning the town to the humans and ensuring that silver would enter folklore forever.

Later, in the 1760s, there is a well-known story involving silver bullets and the previously mentioned Beast of Gévaudan. Jean Chastel, one of the hunters credited with killing the Beast, testified that he shot the loup-garou using silver bullets made from a melted chalice that was blessed by a priest. It is unclear if he believed the silver itself had true significance from older tales such as Greifswald, or if he used the bullets because they were made from a consecrated item that happened to be silver.

Silver is traditionally associated with the moon in occult tradition. It could be that the first person to dream up the idea of using silver weapons against what he or she thought was a werewolf could have gotten the inspiration from a musty grimoire. Let's say that Greifswald really was the first werewolf event where silver was used as a weapon. It's not impossible that a student in 1640 would have read some books on magic.

The line of reasoning used by that student, or maybe an even earlier werewolf hunter, probably evolved from the idea of "like working on like" in the occult world. If wolves hunted by the moon, perhaps a lunar metal had power over wolves as well. Such sympathetic links are an ancient staple of occultism and are in use to this day. Modern practitioners of magic still apply the sympathetic principle when selecting the right color of candles, or scent of incense, or even proper day of working. Yes, even days of the week have associations. Monday is linked with the moon, for example, so it's a wonder that hunters didn't believe a silver bullet would work even better on that day. Such a pondering would have been a valid consideration for a superstitious hunter.

So, we can see why silver might have been used by hunters. Folklore doesn't like to agree with itself, though. For every use of silver as the only tool that will work, there are stories in which silver isn't mentioned and the werewolf meets his or her demise.

MUNDANE METHODS

Despite some of the theories we'll be getting to later on in this book, werewolves were believed by the vast majority of people to be physical creatures made of furry flesh and sharp teeth. As a result, it is not surprising that in most countries the methods for killing or hurting a werewolf were simple methods of brute force. What people didn't take into account is that such methods wouldn't help them distinguish between werewolves and humans, or werewolves and real wolves, depending on which form they attacked.

Torture and Flames

The most popular way to kill a werewolf in the Middle Ages was also the preferred choice of dealing with witches, heretics, and basically anyone who offended the Inquisition. Most werewolves that became infamous were arrested in human form, tried in a court (flawed as it was), and then sentenced to various forms of torture and death. There was no way to really know if these were supernatural beings having their skin peeled away slowly or bones broken on a wheel—no final proof of what torturers killed by beheading or burning at the stake, or both. These were ways to kill people, too!

People back in the Middle Ages didn't know for sure if any of these methods would work against a werewolf while he or she was in wolf form, but they had records of it working every time when the accused was in human form. Note that they never had a chance to try any of these methods when the accused—or sometimes freely confessed—werewolf was in wolf form, because there is not a single court case on record where the prisoner turned into a wolf and tried to pounce out of the courtroom. The explanation offered for this lack of actual evidence didn't bother the courts. Satan simply abandoned his servants once they were captured, including the witches who could somehow kill at a distance but couldn't even stop a single lash of a whip from hitting their backs.

There you have it. In human form, once abandoned by the devil, werewolves can be killed like any other human. The devil must hate courtrooms.

Blades and Boring Bullets

Our best-documented cases of alleged lycanthropy almost always ended in a courtroom. The rest of the legends usually had very vague outcomes, with the implication being that beasts could still be lurking in the woods. However, you went with what you knew must work. If werewolves could be killed in human form by the authorities using any physical weapons and torture devices on hand, then it followed logically that hunters should take to the woods armed with any weapons they'd use against real wolves.

A select few hunters used silver, as already covered, but in practice silver became a generic folk belief rather than something that was a must-have on hunts. You were more likely to find silver mentioned in an old text as something to try, and not as something someone actually tried. It wasn't cheap, after all.

As non-mystical as this fact may be, hunters went in search of werewolves with their ordinary muskets, guns, swords, knives, pitchforks, and other weapons made from more affordable and easy-to-come-by metals.

Telltale Wounds and Lopping Off Paws

A recurring element in folklore is the telltale wound that carries over when a lycanthrope transforms from a wolf back into human form. We first find an example of this about two thousand years ago in Petronius' *Satyricon*, in which a soldier changes into a wolf and is seriously wounded while caught attacking cattle. Once back in human form, he is easily identified by having the same wounds on his body.

Another old tale containing the telltale wound was related by a then-well-known writer who specialized in writing about the bizarre. In the sixteenth century, Bishop Olaus Magnus was the go-to guy if you wanted to learn about everything from sea monsters to, of course, werewolves. If he had been born a few centuries later, he would have made a great cryptozoologist, no doubt. The anecdote of Bishop Magnus comes to us from the Baltic province of Livonia, which we'll hear about again in another werewolf legend in the last chapter of this book. Again, the wound in this story isn't really a way to kill a were-wolf, but rather a way to identify it:

> *The wife of a nobleman in Livonia expressed her doubts to one of her slaves whether it were possible for man or woman thus to change shape. The servant at once volunteered to give her evidence of the possibility. He left the room, and in another moment a wolf was observed running over the country. The dogs followed him, and notwithstanding his resistance, tore out one of his eyes. Next day the slave appeared before his mistress blind of an eye.*[1]

These are not isolated legends. The general concept of the telltale wound has appeared all around the world, perhaps helped along by what a good story it makes: instant proof and terror in an anecdote. Whether a hunter encounters a werewolf while tracking it to protect a village, or an unlucky guy or gal crosses paths with the beast by accident, the idea is the same. The human manages to get a strike in with whatever weapon he or she is carrying, and the beast then flees. Sometimes this is just a gash with a blade; other times the human actually manages to cut off a paw.

In its simplest form, this story element leads to the werewolf's direct capture. The hunter or villager returns to tell others of how he or she cut the beast in a specific part of the body. Someone then claims to have seen another villager with the very same wound on a matching spot—such as hand instead of paw, or ear instead of, well, ear. Of course whenever a wolf part is cut off, the hunter later finds that the paw or other severed wolf part has turned into a hand or another human body part. This transformation occurred sometime after the part was placed in the blade-wielder's pouch.

More entertaining versions of the legend include a villager hearing the tale of the hunter and seeing the actual removed, now-human body part. Something about the severed part looks familiar, such as a ring it has on its finger. The nervous villager then races home, only to find his or her spouse missing a hand.

Other than making one wonder how a ring can stay on during human-to-wolf-to-human transformation cycles, the telltale-wound legends reinforce the idea that flesh-and-blood werewolves can be harmed in much the same way as any flesh-and-blood creature.

EXORCISM

We touched earlier on how Saint Augustine helped along the general belief that the devil had something to do with lycanthropy. Naturally, if the evil one's powers were at work during a transformation, then it wasn't irrational to believe that exorcism could kill or cure a werewolf. Okay, so exorcism is a funny topic to comment on as being rational or irrational, but we're considering the mindset of those living before and during the Middle Ages. Today, a diagnosis of bacterial infection results in an antibiotic prescription as standard procedure. Back in the times when werewolves and other evil beings were believed to roam the world, devilry of one form or another often begat exorcism.

The Burning Times often didn't contain much mercy. By the time a suspected witch or werewolf got to trial, the authorities were not interested in helping him or her be cured. Helping someone be cured of evil was usually undertaken privately, before the person became a local pariah.

In the thirteenth century, before werewolf trials and executions became the choice way of dealing with the "problem," there is an interesting example of a priest taking matters into his own hands when learning of an alleged werewolf in the area. Rather than ordering the suspect brought before a court, this priest apparently challenged the man to turn into a wolf right before him. When the man did so, the priest began his exorcism and cured the werewolf. His theory for doing so was that even though such an evil transformation could take place, it could not corrupt the man's soul inside. It is not clear exactly what kind of exorcism rite was performed, as few details of this event have survived.

A Bizarre Exorcism Rite

A much more detailed example of exorcism comes to us by way of Elliott O'Donnell. He describes in his 1912 book, *Werwolves*, that up until "recent" times, lycanthropy was treated in Russia with exorcism. He goes on to give a ritual that no priest would be able to perform with the sanction of the church, as it resembles something out of a grimoire.

The ritual involves creating a seven-foot magical circle related to Mercury, and containing planetary symbols of that essence drawn around the perimeter. Mercury was selected because the priest believed this intelligence was the "most bitter opponent of all evil spirits." I don't see much occult precedence for favoring this planetary influence so significantly to perform an exorcism. You can make arguments for any of the planets based on how you spin their mythological and traditional attributes to your purpose.

The ritual goes on to suggest adding the following mixture to a pot of water:

> *2 drachms of sulphur*
> *½ oz. of castoreum*
> *6 drachms of opium*
> *3 drachms of asafœtida*
> *½ oz. of hypericum*
> *¾ oz. of ammonia*
> *½ oz. of camphor*[2]

Added to this mixture are a bit of mandrake root, fungus, and living things: namely, a snake and two toads that are tied up in linen bags. The mixture was cruelly brought to a boil. Holding a wand made of bound-together ash, birch, and white poplar, the priest/magician would pray at a makeshift altar in the magic circle until the toads indicated the water had reached a boil, no doubt by making some horrible pained croaks or other sounds.

The priest would then take a cupful of the boiling liquid and use the wand to splash bits of the mixture onto the werewolf. If the latter is in wolf form (or is just a real wolf), I'd imagine it wouldn't take too kindly to the hot liquid. Assuming the priest could somehow get away with splashing this liquid onto the beast, he would utter the following chant three times:

> *In the name of Our Blessed Lady I command thee to depart.*
> *Black, evil devils from Hell, begone!*
> *Begone!*
> *Again I say, begone!*[3]

Allegedly, this worked in a case that would have occurred in the first decade or so of the twentieth century. It is so unlike Christian exorcism, and such an oddity for even the realm of occult lore, that I can't vouch for this rite's authenticity. But if exorcism, too, falls under the category of psychodrama affecting someone who believes in it, then it's easy to accept that it would work just fine on somebody who only *believes* he or she is a werewolf. From the boiling animals, to the strange symbols, to the burning by liquid, the rite certainly is dramatic.

Note: Between this ritual and the one from the preceding chapter, I'm expecting at least some mail from PETA, the ASPCA, and readers who are in league with their principles. Let me try and curb some of that with a disclaimer. No animals were harmed in the making of this book . . . at least none in the last century or so!

The Warrens' Werewolf

Ed and Lorraine Warren are well known in the world of the paranormal. Years before the recent spate of ghost-hunting shows hit TV, the Warrens were appearing on standalone documentaries describing their encounters with the paranormal at clients' homes. For all they did for increasing the TV coverage of paranormal investigations, the Warrens tended toward the sensational in their cases and in the books they published afterward. A typical cover blurb was "Scarier than Stephen King."

While modern paranormal-investigation groups are usually looking for ghosts, the Warrens immediately diagnosed paranormal cases as houses that "need Jesus in them." But this isn't a book on exploring the dangers of going into someone's house—someone whose current mental state you're not sure of—and tossing around terms that imply the devil is behind everything ailing him or her. You'll read much about the powers of psychodrama in these pages, though, and I'll let you draw your own conclusions about why it may not be the best investigative technique to resort to.

On to a well-known werewolf case that the Warrens investigated. This one takes place in London.

A man named Bill Ramsey had a strange experience as a young boy. He said that one sunny day while playing outside he felt as though he'd walked into a meat locker and his core temperature dropped by about 20 degrees. This was accompanied by a foul odor that reminded him of a time when the sewer in the neighborhood backed up. The initial feeling faded, but it left little Bill somehow changed for the rest of his life.

As Ramsey grew into adulthood, he would from time to time feel the compulsion to perform some violent act. Rage would swell in him, and he would even literally snap at others like a dog. In 1983 this reached a peak when he was admitted into a hospital one night, bit his attending nurse, and held onto the bite with relish. He then growled and pounced around on all fours. Ramsey was eventually restrained and committed to a psychiatric ward.

The Warrens descended on the case and decided that this man was possessed by a werewolf demon. They invited Bishop Robert Mc-Kenna to come and exorcise the demon. Unlike the bizarre exorcism ritual we examined earlier, this was a straightforward rite of the type you've seen in movies, but with much less supernatural fanfare and no pea-soup emissions. Ramsey tried to lash out a couple of times during the rite, but that's it.

He did claim to have felt something leave his body when the exorcism was completed, but Ramsey hasn't been talking about the experience since. The psychodrama may have worked in this case, which is good for Ramsey and his family—and a testament to the power of exorcism on someone who believes it may help.

FOLKLORE'S "SIMPLE" CURES

You didn't need to be a man of the cloth to help someone out of his or her werewolf state, it seems. People in almost every region that harbored the belief in shapeshifters had at least one nonviolent cure. Actually, some are not exactly peaceful, so perhaps *nonlethal* is a better word to describe these werewolf folk cures.

Voluntarily Opting Out

If you're a voluntary werewolf, the most obvious cure for lycanthropy is to stop doing whatever it is you're doing to become a wolf in the first place. Stop rubbing on that salve, maybe leave the wolf skin on the coat hook next full moon. The werewolves on trial admitted that they could take off the skin and become human again . . . until the next time they put the skin on.

This isn't much of a werewolf cure, of course, because if you're so obsessed with having the powers in the first place, chances are you won't want to give them up for no good reason. It seems the only time that a werewolf is cured by not doing the voluntary ritual acts that turn him or her into a werewolf is when others intervene. For example, when Jean Grenier was locked away in the insane asylum, the authorities didn't provide him with his salve and wolf skin. You can argue that this didn't exactly cure him, considering that during his follow-up visit he was still acting quite mad. You can take the tools away from the voluntary werewolf, but you can't remove the wolf nature from the voluntary werewolf's mind.

Bloody Folk Cures

Ah, blood. You can't discuss the dark creatures of folklore without this red liquid coming up repeatedly. While mundane folk cures involved doing things like blowing on something three times, or saying something three times, werewolf-related folk cures seemed to always involve drawing blood from the beast somehow . . . and, yes, it had to be done three times in some examples.

The most common quick cure is to hit the werewolf three times on the top of the head, ensuring that each strike draws at least a drop of blood. Perhaps the thinking was that the werewolf would be able to see or smell its own blood and remember its humanity. Trying this cure could be perilous, of course. First of all, you'd have to strike quickly enough to get all three hits in before the wolf kindly relieved you of the hand doing the striking. Second, and probably most dangerous of all, was the horrible outcome even if you did manage to get all three strikes in, only to find you were facing an ordinary, and now incredibly angry, wolf.

In Italy it was believed that one X-shaped cut to the head would do the trick. The same disclaimers about what may happen afterward apply.

An equally dangerous folk cure was to cut the wolf on the back of its front paws. This could also be explained as a way to get the wolf to smell its own blood, or could have developed from the telltale-wound legends we examined earlier. After all, those hunters went so far as to cut off a paw, and the wolf did retreat and turn back into human form. Those stories don't include a true cure, though, just a temporary return to human form to allow for the dramatic reveal of the wound. Again, cutting at the paw of a real wolf would have a most unpleasant outcome.

Here, Wolfy, I Mean, Wally

Another folk cure relies on reminding a werewolf of his or her human nature. This one involves being able to identify who the werewolf really is and addressing him or her by the known human name. Being a folk cure, the preferred way to do this was to call out the name three times.

Werewolf lore is full of unnameable, untraceable anecdotes, and the name-recognition belief is no exception. An unnamed farmer was supposedly out in his field one day when a large wolf appeared and attacked his horse. For some reason, the farmer recognized the particular behavior and mannerisms of the wolf and yelled out, asking if the wolf was his mother. The wolf transformed back into his mother after that. A strange way to recognize Mom, for sure, but it worked according to this tale. Had the wolf been his mother-in-law instead of his mother, we might have finally known where that particular stereotype evolved.

Other legends seem to indicate that you don't necessarily need to know the werewolf's name, only that it is no ordinary wolf. Just yelling at the beast, claiming that you are aware it is a werewolf, may do the trick. I like this folk cure. It is less likely to irritate a real wolf than, say, cutting or rapping on its head.

Even throwing pieces of human clothes at a werewolf, whether the beast owns them or not, is said to remind it of its nature. This cure could also just give the wolf a fresh scent to go after. These folk cures really are trouble! Want more proof of that? Read on.

Not Quite an Exorcism

Magic charms are often quite charming to read, and some achieve immortality in pop culture. A notable example is the overused ABRACADABRA, which was once a cure for various illnesses and is now uttered as rabbits are pulled out of hats in cartoons. While not as popular, a couple of simple charms designed to kick a wolf "spirit" out of a man or woman survive, and are worth including here.

The first puts three young girls in peril as they are asked to circle the werewolf, and throw ash twigs at it while it is in wolf form, while chanting:

> *Gray wolf ugly, gray wolf old,*
> *Do at once as you are told.*
> *Leave this man and fly away—*
> *Right away, far away,*
> *Where it's night and never day.*[4]

You get the idea how insane some of these cures would be to try if the beast is either a real wolf or, heck, a werewolf that really needs a dose of silver bullets instead! But if throwing twigs at a wolf doesn't seem irritating and dangerous enough, we'll close the chapter with this folk cure:

Go, fly, away to the sky.
Devilish graywolf, we do thee defy.
Out, out, out, with a howl and a yell
That will carry you faster and surer to Hell.[5]

Seems threatening enough. Surely the werewolf will obey. Oh, did I mention you're supposed to repeatedly kick the wolf while chanting the above?

Yup. Good, safe fun, that one.

CHAPTER SEVEN

MODERN
SIGHTINGS

Both types of flesh-and-blood were-wolves have made themselves known so far. We've examined how to become them, and destroy them. Of course, the context of all these descriptions is hardly current. The first half of this book very much focused on yesteryear.

Have werewolves been seen in the modern day? With vampires, folkloric-type blood drinkers seemed to vanish in current times. You can argue that embalming has destroyed the undead before they could rise, or obviously that the undead never existed. Either way, vampires of the risen-dead type just don't seem to pop up on current supernatural radar. As I cover in *Vampires: The Occult Truth*, only psychic vampires seem to have any presence in the modern day. The castle-dwellers aren't showing us their capes, it seems. But their cinematic companions, werewolves, didn't seem to get the memo that it's not okay to appear in the modern world.

You're about to read accounts of some uncannily recent sightings of furry beings. We'll move from military eyewitnesses in Europe during the twentieth century to even more recent accounts from around the United States. Much more recent. As hard to believe as it may be, we'll examine accounts from the twenty-first century!

WEREWOLF SHRINE

If you're going to trust a modern eyewitness to a werewolf sighting, believing several of them from the Air Force doesn't seem like a bad way to go. Just such a group claims to have seen something unexplainable in the Morbach region of Germany in 1988. What's most interesting is the region has a werewolf legend all its own.

First the backstory to the local legend. It was the time of Napoleon, and a deserter from his army, one Thomas Schwytzer, fled the battlefront in Russia with a group of soldiers. On their way back home, the hungry soldiers found a small farmhouse near Wittlich—a German town, though at the time incorporated into Napoleon's expansionist French state—and looted the property in hopes of finding something to eat. The farmer who owned the farmhouse, along with his sons, tried to stop the soldiers, but the war-ravaged and starved soldiers quickly killed the male residents in cold blood.

Before they left, the soldiers also encountered the farmer's wife. She stared down Schwytzer, and in her agony uttered a curse at him, telling him that at each full moon he would change into a form befitting his savagery—into a wolf. Likely not taking her seriously, Schwytzer killed her too, and left the farmhouse.

According to Wittlich legend, though, the curse did take effect. While starvation and temporary war insanity may have affected his actions that night at the farmhouse, Schwytzer soon became a ravenous fellow. Abandoning the other soldiers, he stayed in the area and became a local criminal plague on the area, robbing folks and hiding in the forest. At least that's what he did when the moon wasn't full. People soon started seeing a large wolflike beast, and both humans and livestock began to go missing.

While we have no solid eyewitness accounts from the time, it may be that the soldiers whom Schwytzer deserted told others in the area about the wife's curse. Suggestibility may have turned the wild bandit of the woods into a werewolf in the eyes of the locals.

It may have been an all-too-human action that did Schwytzer in, however. Schwytzer raped a farmer's daughter named Elizabeth Beierle and let her get away. A few nights later, a group of villagers hunting for either the werewolf or the rapist (it is unclear) came across Schwytzer's campsite and decide to take matters into their own hands. Schwytzer tried to flee but only made it as far as the village of Morbach, where the mob killed him.

The mob buried Schwytzer at a crossroads and built a small shrine. They believed that as long as a candle remained lit on the shrine, the werewolf would not rise and come back. Elizabeth Beierle went on to give birth to Schwytzer's son, but he and his descendants never transformed or exhibited any of their ancestor's evil behavior. Peace and normalcy had returned to the area. Many years later, a U.S. Air Force base was even built in the Morbach area, then part of West Germany.

Which brings us back to 1988, and to that group of men in uniform returning to base one night.

Small towns with a single legend to share usually share it with everyone, including the military. All the men in the group knew all about the shrine and what it was supposed to prevent the return of. Just one problem: the candle wasn't lit as they passed it.

They found it funny, telling each other that the werewolf would surely return now. If this was a horror movie, you'd expect a howl to erupt and all the men to meet a horrible fate before managing to return to their base. That didn't exactly happen, but the night was not without its horror movie-type scene.

The group made it back to the base without encountering any werewolves. However, in the middle of the night something did set off the sensors on the base's outside fence. Something was either lurking out there . . . or had already breached the perimeter!

A dispatched security unit went to investigate and found something you don't normally see inside a military base. Members of the security unit described the intruder as being a huge wolflike creature that stood upright. The creature didn't attack the guards, despite being close to them and on the same side of the fence. Rather, it only stared them down and leaped the almost eight-foot-high fence to disappear into the woods.

The beast was never found that night. Trying to use search dogs to follow it was no use. The dogs wouldn't follow the scent, whimpering out of fear.

After this story began circulating, other soldiers came forth from the base, claiming to have seen the beast as well. A different guard said he encountered the beast one night, believing it stood nearly eight feet tall. He claimed that the creature jumped a different twelve-foot fence.

The second account can either lend credibility to the tale or just prove that things get better with the retelling. No physical evidence exists to validate either encounter, making it a modern piece of folklore.

AN AMERICAN WEREWOLF IN ... WISCONSIN

Since 1936, people in Wisconsin have occasionally claimed to see a large, human-sized, bulky beast that walks upright. Of course, besides being furry, it is also said to have the head of a wolf. Maybe because they were afraid of being called insane, eyewitnesses of this beast didn't make much of a big deal over it. Until 1989, not even serious Bigfoot freaks or other types of cryptozoology fans gave Wisconsin much thought. It just remained below the radar, like that weird rumor floating around your town that I and a couple hundred million other folks in America have never heard about.

All this changed one night with a sighting that would soon capture national attention.

It was the wee hours of a fall morning, about 1:30 a.m., when a waitress who worked in a bar in Elkhorn was driving home from her shift. This woman, Lori Endrizzi, was taking a dark road that would soon after become synonymous with werewolves in America: Bray Road.

Lori's headlights reflected back two eerie points that turned out to be eyes. The thing to which the eyes belonged was brownish-gray and just under six feet tall. It was busy eating some kind of roadkill, and as it looked at Lori in the headlights, she could see that it had claws, sharp teeth, and, of course, a wolflike face, complete with a snout and pointy ears. And it was confident, evidently, as it did not flee from Lori's headlights. Eating its roadkill was definitely more important.

A similar if not identical beast was spotted a couple of years later on, appropriately enough, Halloween in 1991. Doris Gipson, a high-school student, ventured down mysterious Bray Road. She thought her car rose up for an instant as if she hit something, so she stopped. Getting out to examine the road, Doris started walking back. She never got to validate if she hit something small, however, as something huge was running toward her, possibly coming for her fresh roadkill.

The thing's description matched Lori's, being a tall, furry creature with a wolf head. Doris got back in her car as quickly as she could, but she claims the thing did reach her vehicle before she got away. There were long claw scratches on the rear of the car to prove it!

After these stories hit the wires, amateur werewolf hunters from around the country began descending on this and nearby areas in hopes of seeing the Beast of Bray Road. Either to get attention or because they finally felt safe to admit it, various people came forward and claimed to have had experiences before one or both of the aforementioned Bray Road sightings. A good example is a farmer named Mike Etten, who in 1990 said he saw something big and furry on Bray Road one night. Assumption kicked in and he thought it was a bear, but now that he thought of it, the shape of the head did seem more canine to him.

All the activity of the media and amateurs (okay, so there aren't really any professional werewolf hunters) seems to have scared the creature away. For the time being, all we have to go on are the old, pre–media frenzy sightings. And their similarities certainly are hard to ignore.

Before we abandon this particular creature, recall how in 1936 someone saw the beast as well. The description then was roughly the same, with a man-sized bulky beast that had a roughly wolflike head. That eyewitness, Mark Schackelman, claimed to have seen it digging in an Indian mound. This could mean nothing, but it could be significant. We'll have more to say about Native American werewolf beliefs in chapter 9.

THE HOWLING IN UPSTATE NEW YORK

The following experience was shared with me by a professor at a college in upstate New York. I'm guessing he didn't feel this story would "compute" with his colleagues, as he agreed to share the experience only under the assurance of anonymity. I of course agreed. As I have verified his identity, I can say with some certainty that he doesn't seem like the type to make up an experience like this. I'm delighted to be able to share his experience here in print for the first (and likely only) time:

Returning from dinner at a colleague's house one night in November 2008, I noticed my tire-pressure light was on. It was just west of the town where I live [omitted by request], and I was debating trying to ride the flat tire home. As my steering pulled more and more to the right, and the sound grew increasingly awful, I decided instead to start looking for a well-lit, flat spot to try and perform what would be my first tire change. I'm not a car guy.

I started to pull over onto a particular curve in the road that looked promising. I never stopped fully, however. My headlights illuminated something running with what I can only describe as a lope. The thing was hunched over and practically bouncing as it moved along. The effect was of something burly moving quickly, then stopping as if to examine something on the ground, then moving quickly again. I had never seen anything move quite like that, and couldn't identify what it was. I was not comfortable getting out of the car, and equally uncomfortable listening to the grinding sound of my wheel again if I got on the road. So I waited a moment, more curious than afraid.

Then the thing turned around and looked in my direction. It was just to the left of my headlights' main cone of illumination. I could still see the shape of its head, though. It had triangular ears and a face that was unusually wide. I think it was excessive fur coming out of the sides of its head, but I can't be sure. I am certain it had a long snout, though. It was as if the world's largest wolf had its head transplanted onto the body of an ape.

These details all became clearer over time. A full two minutes must have passed with us locked in that stare, as an entire block of commercials on the radio played out with my barely registering any of them. When the commercials ended it snapped my nerve, and I decided to risk venturing onto the road again. Almost as if it read my mind, the thing turned and continued with its lope. I snapped off the radio and tried to process what I had just seen. It vanished into the dark. An instant later I heard a howl unlike anything I'd ever heard come from an animal. It almost sounded like a mixture of breaking wood and a howl.

Needless to say, I called AAA and stayed in my car. I still haven't changed a tire and don't plan on doing so if I ever have another flat on that road.

Besides giving me an interesting stretch of road to hit next time I'm in the mood for a road trip, this professor's tale seems to describe the same type of beast from the Wisconsin accounts in appearance. Wish he could have taped that howl. The mixture he describes is fascinating.

GROWLING, NORTH OF THE BORDER

I get lots of mail from people who have had paranormal experiences, and I was pleased to come across another werewolf type of experience from a location bordering on New York state. It's always fun to have things to check out that are just a drive away. Okay, this one is even farther north than the professor's experience, so it would be quite a drive, but it could be worth it:

Where I'm from [the Canadian side of the Niagara Region] there is a great deal of residual energy due to the history of this area. Some of it is very rural, and it is in those areas that you encounter the most activity. Friends of mine were driving back late from viewing a home basically out in the middle of nowhere. On the way they could see something running alongside the car—just a shadow, but very big. When they got home, it was gone.

Later they went out for a smoke and could hear growling and scratching noises. Then something heavy jumped on their car and was coming towards where they were sitting. They thought it was the same shadow from on the road earlier, and they ran inside and called me. I'm a sensitive, and always have been since I was child, so most people who know me call me when they encounter something strange.

We drove out to the location where they first saw the shadow thing. It wasn't long before we saw it again, this time in what they thought was better detail. It looked like a large dog or wolf, but not right in its appearance. It was like a gray shadow. It followed the car again, back to their place. We sat outside till it got dark, then walked to about where they had heard it the previous night.

Sitting there, we could hear it growling and scratching. Then it walked past us to the woods behind their house. It was the spirit of a werewolf, I believe. I say this because later we could hear it trying to speak to us, like it was trapped in both human and animal spirit forms. It was incredible to see and feel something like that. It is still there most times, making noise but never causing any issues with neighboring animals or people. If you are ever in Canada, you should look up the history in the Niagara Region.

As with the Morbach werewolf, this sighting is believed to be something human that has passed yet has an animal spirit form. Is it possible for a spirit to take on a form like this? I'll have more to say on shapeshifting without a physical body when we discuss astral werewolves in chapter 11.

SNIPPETS OF SNOUTS AROUND THE USA

Turns out we've had quite a few sightings of furry ones here in America, some of them lesser known. These come from various sources, but do combine to create an interesting bundle of experiences.

One worth noting is a tale related in *Fate* magazine in 1960. Mrs. Delburt Gregg of Texas claimed that she saw a huge wolflike creature staring at her through her window. It was a stormy night, and she could see its mouth full of sharp teeth illuminated by lightning, almost as if this were straight out of a bad horror movie. What makes the brief account interesting is that the eyewitness in this case tried to visually follow the beast as it ran off into the bushes. Using her flashlight, she scanned the brush. A wolf never emerged, but a tall man did! He hurried down the road and never returned, that she knows of. Unlike the other experiences in this chapter, this one implies that the woman saw a werewolf while he was in his creature form, then after he changed into human. Or she tied two unrelated sightings together, as has been done in the past with people encountered in the woods.

Michigan has had legends of a "dogman" in its woods for several years. The general idea of animal-human hybrids has existed in the area for centuries, dating back to Native Americans who believed in the possibility. Curiously, there even was a group of Native American soldiers in the nineteenth century called the Cheyenne Dog Soldiers, although it is unclear if they believed in shapeshifting. One eyewitness report from 1999 describes the thing as being about the size of a bear, with wolf eyes and an elongated head.

Henrico County, Virginia, has a local legend of a six-foot, grayish werewolf that howls at the full moon. It has been described as running both upright and on all fours, and eyewitnesses claim to have been chased by it. As expected, none of these eyewitnesses were caught, hence their ability to be eyewitnesses.

Another experience comes from one of my readers living in Ohio:

I was twelve years old in 1988. I lived in Cleveland, Ohio, with my grandparents. My bedroom window looked out onto the street, giving me a clear view of the front gate to our yard. It was night, and as I lay on my bed this snarling-type sound cut through the quiet. I walked over to my window to peer out and see if I could spot anything. I could see a man's silhouette that was crouching down and kind of frantically moving about. Think of a caged wild man type of movement. Anyway, something told me that this wasn't normal, and I shouldn't let this "man" know that I was watching. As he turned to face my house, it looked like he fell onto all fours and ran toward the alley that was behind our house. Not a minute after, I heard a dog howl. I can still remember how hard my heart was beating. I didn't see him after that night, but I have always wondered what he or it was.

I don't have much to go on, so I have to wonder the same thing.

Another experience from the region happened in 1972, in Defiance, Ohio. Three separate witnesses sighted a humanoid creature that had a furry body and a wolflike head. The descriptions varied slightly, and some included fangs, but some also included . . . blue jeans! That's right, just like in the werewolf movies in which pants don't rip off during the transformation process (likely in order to keep a decent MPAA rating). This wolf man attacked a railroad worker with a long two-by-four plank—probably the only werewolf of legends old or new to wield a club, or any other type of weapon for that matter, against its victims. No one was ever caught, so the sightings were never explained away as, say, the perpetrator being a crazy human wearing a mask.

One last experience is interesting because it places an alleged werewolf in a graveyard, as in Native American beliefs. This one hails from a reader of mine in Lake Stevens, Washington, in the Pacific Northwest. Out of all the letters I've received, I believe this one features the only white-wolf creature in the bunch:

I did see one and no one believes me, but I know what I saw. Hence the absolute obsession I seem to have with them since that night.

I was getting ready to pull into a graveyard late at night and as I turned into the drive my headlights scanned over the grounds. I saw a rather large white dog, or I thought that's what it was, illuminated there.

Well, it was crouched over a grave so naturally I was instantly fascinated with whatever this thing was. I parked and kept my lights on it. It turned to look in my direction and that's when I noticed its face. It was neither beast nor man, but half and half. We stared at each other for a moment and then it got up. Yes, it stood up and just walked off on two legs into the woods, pausing to look back once more before disappearing slowly into the trees.

Normally someone's reaction would be to turn tail out of there, but not me. I got out of my car and walked toward the woods, pausing to see what grave it had been at. It was that of a child. I walked closer still to the woods. I never saw it again but I could feel it watching me. I felt no negative feelings, just a sort of calm like I knew it would never hurt me.

I have since then gone back to that graveyard several times, but I have never seen it again. I would say it was roughly 5'1". Basically like a white dog with something human about the way it walked and its face. Anyway that's my experience. I just wanted you to know about it.

WHAT ARE THEY SEEING?

As the werewolves of legend mostly resembled ordinary wolves, perhaps just larger or more ferocious looking, it's peculiar that a good number of the sightings from the last few decades feature creatures that resemble humanoid werewolves. Back in the day when people lived in close proximity to and in perceived danger from real wolves, it was horrible enough to imagine a man or woman turning into one of these things and having a preternatural bloodlust. Since then, horror movies have stepped in to turn werewolves into large, anthropomorphic beasts that cannot be mistaken for real wolves. Alleged sightings have likewise become a whole lot more in line with what is portrayed on film.

This type of appearance-fits-the-era phenomenon is not unique to werewolves. While I'm not really a UFO buff, I still find it curious that you can take accounts of alien abductees and often sort them by decade and the visitors' associated appearances. The familiar large-head, large-black-eyes look of pop culture is now almost exclusively what abductees report seeing. Before this agreed-upon look for extraterrestrials entered mainstream consciousness via TV and films, however, aliens were described as being of literally all shapes and sizes. Some even looked like anthropomorphic, furry creatures with pointy ears and large heads.

Not going there!

CHAPTER EIGHT

MODERN MEDICINE

Finding ordinary explanations for some of the sightings we just discussed could prove difficult. Most of them do seem to involve flesh-and-blood type creatures, but not creatures that should exist according to modern zoology. If what the eyewitnesses say is true, then the folklore doesn't seem so far-fetched. Too bad there's little if any evidence to support the modern accounts. A scratch on a car will not revolutionize modern science's view on lycanthropy.

We may need to look elsewhere for explanations of physical werewolves. This book wouldn't be balanced if we didn't also focus on some of the modern medical explanations for lycanthropy that may account for the legends. Few people seem to know that lycanthropy is actually found in modern psychological literature, and is a puzzling but recognized mental disorder. Also, there are physical conditions that, due to either extra hairiness or other disfigurements, may have led superstitious villagers to believe they had come face to face with an animal-human hybrid.

CLINICAL LYCANTHROPY

The case of Jean Grenier marked the approximate start of leniency and reason in werewolf court cases. Despite hearing a story that was familiar in court records, the officials decided that this time around the salve, wolf girdle, and admissions of guilt may not have meant that the devil was afoot. Grenier was ruled insane, and as a later visit to his monastery showed, that was a rare good call on the part of the court. Even without his magical implements, Grenier remained obsessed with the idea of being a wolf, and acted anything but sane in his last days.

They Sort of Knew it Existed

What's most amazing about clinical lycanthropy is that medical practitioners in the second century CE knew of it. You read that right. A good 1,400 years before the first court decisions of leniency toward people who thought they were werewolves, and over a thousand years before mania and fear erupted, a doctor by the name of Marcellus of Sida not only wrote about clinical lycanthropy, but also tried to apply the medicine of the day toward getting a cure.

Marcellus gave a few odd physical traits for his lycanthropes, including a listless gaze, dry tongue and eyes, and gauntness. However, his real contribution was that he called lycanthropy a form of melancholy or a mental disorder. He even had a bizarre cure, involving bloodletting and days of baths with various substances, finishing off with sleep-inducing drugs. His techniques were as odd as those of his time (bloodletting was used for nearly all ailments), but his insight that it was a mental disorder can't be ignored. As we delve deeper into clinical lycanthropy and how complicated its causes may be, we can see that Marcellus was not ahead of his time in the curing department. But he was a pioneer in recognizing a type of madness for what it was.

A sixteenth-century Dutch man of medicine also knew how to spot madness for what it was in lycanthropy cases. This doctor, Petrus Forestus, identified a particular peasant who every spring would run around in a wild state in a local church and cemetery. Interestingly, he was covered with the types of scars that Marcellus predicted would appear in most cases of lycanthropy. Forestus knew this man to be a lycanthrope of the clinical type, perhaps because Forestus had read Marcellus' words. We can't be sure how he knew, but the point remains that the courts had at their disposal papers written by so-called esteemed men of science.

Spotting the Signs

It's hard to conceive of how many folkloric werewolves only suffered from a form of clinical lycanthropy. Even today you can't in all cases point to something in a patient and determine that he or she has an isolated case of clinical lycanthropy. Psychological disorders are not always clear-cut, and do not always present themselves alone. Separating the symptoms from the causes can be a challenge.

The most obvious indication that someone may be suffering from clinical lycanthropy is the freely admitted belief that he or she changes into a werewolf. A good example of what might have been a clinical lycanthrope from yesteryear is a particular peasant who, in human form, killed several people and tore them apart. He was captured in 1541 in Pavia, Italy. Although his name is lost to history, he has the particular notoriety of claiming at his trial that he was a werewolf whose fur grew on the *inside*. Considering how heinous his murders were, the peasant was cruelly appeased by the court. They spared no time cutting him open in several places to see if he was telling the truth, but found no fur. Of course, psychology wasn't the only kind of medicine that was in its infancy in the day, and the peasant did not survive.

If he was a clinical lycanthrope, his fur did figuratively grow inside . . . inside his mind.

Today, clinical lycanthropes are usually diagnosed after they exhibit two major indicators. The first is their behaving like a wolf or other animal, and that can be dramatic to behold. The second is that they often can exit this mental state for a while and display awareness of their condition, almost like a werewolf in a movie who confesses to thinking he did something terrible in wolf form the night before.

What could cause this condition? For all our increasing knowledge of the science of the mind, and our understanding of how neurotransmitters and chemical imbalances may affect behavior, we still have no definite explanation for what could make someone feel he or she is a wolf or other animal (*zoanthropy* is the term used when a patient believes he or she changes into other animal forms). But we are getting closer with recent advances.

Having a Good Sense of Body Image

Doctors studying the condition quickly came to the conclusion that clinical lycanthropy may have something to do with how patients perceive themselves. Lycanthropy would not be alone in exploiting such a flaw; the human mind has proven to betray us in this respect with numerous other conditions. For example, some people feel they're way too fat even moments before dying of anorexia. This kind of psychological condition, where a sufferer is concerned with a defect he or she *believes* is found in his or her body, is called *body dysmorphic disorder* (BDD), or *body dysmorphia*. Could something similar to BDD be at work with lycanthropy—some warped perception of appearance or physical nature that ventures into more animalistic imagined defects?

In a 1999 paper entitled "Lycanthropy: New Evidence of Its Origin," Dr. Hamdy F. Moselhy reveals the details of a study that examined the regions of the brain that control proprioception, or one's sense of the relative positions of the body. What Dr. Moselhy postulates is that we may be able to learn something about lycanthropes by analyzing their proprioception regions, including the cerebellum. He used neuroimaging techniques to analyze these regions in two clinical lycanthropes and found conclusive evidence to suggest unusual activity. Put simply, the parts of their brain that tell them they are humans of ordinary shape and size are misfiring. What could cause these anomalies is still unknown.

Even if we find what causes one's sense of body image to be skewed from reality, we would still likely be faced with another puzzle. Why should such an anomaly manifest as a belief that one is turning into a wolf? There aren't people walking around who think they're turning into buildings or trees. But wolves and a few other animals, including cats and birds, come up repeatedly. Rarely, sufferers will feel as if they transform from one animal shape to another.

The principle of atavism may play a role here. Some people have genetic traits that reappear from a distant past. These throwbacks are atavistic traits. Long canine teeth could be a genetic regression to a trait of ancient ancestors, as could extra nipples. Maybe our tendency to imagine we are animals is an extreme genetic throwback down the evolutionary ladder. A similar theory was proposed by Cesare Lombroso in the 1870s to explain criminal behavior, but it never really caught on. Atavism as an explanation is speculation, but worth mentioning as a possible differentiator to why sufferers of the condition are called lycanthropes and not something even stranger like skyscraperthropes.

True Schizophrenia

Notice the word *true* in this subsection's title. Ask most people on the street what the word *schizophrenia* means, and they'll tell you that it's a person with multiple personalities. Everybody knows that. Surely you've heard jokes like: "I have schizophrenia, and so do I." Let's just say that scientists have nothing to do with creating popular jokes.

In fact, schizophrenia has nothing to do with multiple personalities.

Schizophrenia is a disorder in which a patient exhibits distorted perceptions of reality. Such fabricated perceptions can manifest in all five senses, although the most common symptoms of schizophrenia are visual and auditory hallucinations. "Because the voices told me to" is a more apt, if politically incorrect, phrase to describe this disorder than the "so do I" joke is.

It could be that some lycanthropes actually suffer from schizophrenia and happen to randomly imagine wolves or other animals just often enough for the idea to consciously take hold. Wolves in particular are striking, dramatic creatures, and "seeing" one would stand out in memory. Were a patient to imagine the sound of a door slamming, then rain that isn't present, he or she would not be affected in any dramatic way (unless it was the person's first hallucinatory episode). Now, imagine after such mundane hallucinations that the patient is hungry and hears a howling wolf in his or her head. Such a seemingly trivial coincidence could be noticed and "take hold" in a powerful way.

I am not a psychologist, but I'm not exactly rambling here either. Medical theories explaining lycanthropy have been put forth by the professionals. I'm only simplifying their work here to make the possible explanations accessible. The theories seem highly intuitive, though, adhering to the principle of Occam's razor: simple explanations are often the best. There's nothing complex about connecting the disorder of imagining things and the idea that perhaps there's fur growing on the back of your hands.

Dissociative Identity Disorder

Again, schizophrenia is not *multiple personality disorder* (MPD). Actually, MPD is not really MPD any longer. The more commonly used term is *dissociative identity disorder*, or DID, and it actually is a reasonable explanation for some cases of clinical lycanthropy.

One little caveat before we delve into DID. For some doctors, DID is controversial. These professionals argue that everyone dissociates to some degree, and that extreme dissociation has to be an act. For example, next time you have nothing to do, pretend for a minute that the "you" who shows his or her face at school or work is having a conversation with the "you" who has dinner with the family. If you give it a little while and really try to re-create these two (or any other two) faces that you have to put on in life, and let the dialogue flow, the results may be unsettling. Don't worry, no one has "split" into two identities as a result of this exercise. (Or have we?)

In all seriousness, I try to make light of this disease because I'm not truly detached from it. DID has affected someone very close to me, although I'm not at liberty to share more. Suffice it to say that the following information is a combination of research and personal observations.

For a disease that is controversial and difficult for some doctors to accept, DID has an agreed-upon cause or origin as far as the accepting doctors are concerned. Patients who suffer from DID have most often experienced some type of trauma, usually at a young age, which caused their consciousness to fragment or dissociate. The trauma is often sexually abusive in nature, but can also be a result of some other violent action. Such dissociation does not always become apparent to the individual right away; its traits may manifest immediately after the initial trauma, but could remain latent for years.

The traits we're talking about are the emergence of one or more alternative personalities or "alters," which were created by the dissociation. Interviews with these alters when they're in control of the host body usually reveal their feelings about wanting to protect the main personality from memories of the traumatic event, or to prevent the main personality from experiencing similar situations in the future. They call each other by name usually, resulting in eerie statements. For example, say an alter was named Chase, and was a ruffian of sorts. She might comment on why she recently took control: "Jane couldn't handle what her boyfriend said to her, so I had to step in and kick his ass." How long such a takeover would last would depend on how safe things felt for the host personality to be able to safely return.

Occasionally, an alter is unusually primal or animal-like. This could be due to a particularly brutal trauma that caused the initial dissociation, or could arise when the first-created alter isn't effective at protecting the host personality. It's not uncommon for DID sufferers to gradually create new alters in response to life challenges they face. Critics have a hard time disputing how realistic and consistent alters can be in cases where even six or more are present. It almost stretches the limits of human acting ability to consciously handle such switches.

DID patients can be aware of their alters' actions to varying degrees. Some patients claim they watch, helpless, when they're not in the driver's seat, so to speak. Some patients, however, exhibit fugue states in which they can remember none of their actions while they're not in control. Neither sounds particularly pleasant, but it's difficult to imagine a more frightening form of the condition than the fugue states. Imagine "waking up" in a strange location with no recollection of how you got there or what you may have done in the minutes or even hours that have passed.

The basic conditions of lycanthropy, of acting like a wolf and being able to talk about it later, certainly match up to cases of DID where one of the alters is a blatantly primal being. In such cases, the primal alter may act as if it is something nonhuman, and another, more rational alter would take on a role of observing this behavior internally and discussing it with anyone who asks later on. That an alter can be aware of other alters is fascinating, as such information can be shared in a fugue state of its own without the host personality even being aware of the discussion.

Severe cases of DID with multiple alters are not common, but neither is clinical lycanthropy. As a result, DID is certainly a possible medical explanation for "transformative" behavior.

DID has also been put forth as a possible explanation of demonic possession, although I have a strong opinion that such theories are flawed. Here's why. To cure someone of DID, you need to integrate them—a controversial process (yes, everything with DID is controversial). Integration involves getting all the alters to blend together into the host personality, with the theory being that any strengths they possess would then be added to the host to avoid any further need for the alters to exist.

The cure for demonic possession is an exorcism. Even if such a ritual is just psychodrama, as I've hinted at in chapter 6, the drama clearly involves getting rid of an inhabiting personality. DID has never been cured by telling an alter to shove off, to Hell or anywhere else. Therefore, it stands to reason that an exorcism wouldn't cure someone of DID, no matter how strong the belief in the ritual would be.

In summary, if DID results in a lycanthropic alter, the person would have to assimilate that animal nature into himself or herself at some point in order to be cured.

HYPERTRICHOSIS

We now leave the realm of the mind for a moment and delve into mass perception and assumption. People freely associate what they see and don't understand with, well, what they've never seen and don't understand. What would people living five hundred years ago think about a person they encountered who was covered in hair, and looked very much like our wolf man of modern cinema?

Hypertrichosis is a condition in which abnormally excessive amounts of hair grow on a person's body. This can be mild, bordering on someone just being a little hirsute, or severe, with nearly total coverage. The latter type of case can be startling to someone who's not anticipating it. Put yourself back in the Middle Ages for a moment. If you were to hear that wild animals, possibly a wolf, had killed someone in your village, and then you encountered a stranger with hypertrichosis, who knows what conclusions you would have drawn?

But that's pretty much where the similarity lies between someone with this condition and a werewolf of lore. There is no known medical correlation between hypertrichosis and murderous rampages. While it's possible that someone with the disease could have been ostracized and driven to the point of insanity, that's possible with almost anyone who is considered different. Sadly, this kind of ostracizing still happens today, usually resulting in public shootings in a place relevant to where the humiliation took place. And these people driven to the brink rarely have something as severe as hypertrichosis separating them from the "in" folks. Still, the situation that caused the person to be treated differently or bullied is not medically linked to the person's behavior. The bullying itself does the trick.

We postulated what would happen if, during the Middle Ages, an individual ran into someone with hypertrichosis at exactly the wrong moment. Considering how rare the condition is, though, this seems highly unlikely. The most likely reason hypertrichosis has been used frequently by others as an explanation is that it's a convenient-looking explanation to tag on long after lycanthropy mania died down. Consider that an entire family was documented as having this condition in 1648. Granted, it's about fifty years after people started cooling down with werewolf mania, but it's still interesting that with few medical advances in that half-century, no one thought to accuse the man and his children of being monsters. In later centuries, those with the condition ended up in sideshows. So-called "freaks" of the hairy type were a staple in sideshows right until that entertainment form began to lose its appeal in the later decades of the twentieth century.

PORPHYRIA— IT'S NOT JUST FOR VAMPIRES ANYMORE

When I first learned about porphyria years ago, it seemed like a decent fit for at least one misguided explanation of vampirism. Sufferers of this incredibly rare disease have extreme sensitivity to light and equally notable iron deficiencies in their blood. Further, their teeth begin to rot in a bizarre fashion, forming what could be mistaken for really battered, brown fangs if you saw them in the darkness. Of course, porphyriacs can't drink blood to successfully make up for their deficiency, and they really don't exhibit any physical traits that would cause anyone to believe they were powerful supernatural creatures like vampires. As with hypertrichosis, porphyria seemed like a convenient but inadequate explanation to tag on to a legend. Or legends, as we'll get to in a brief moment.

Funny thing about the rare disease (did I mention it's rare?), is that an alarming number of vampire fans claim to have it. I've yet to meet a porphyriac who exhibits a single symptom, but who am I to doubt someone claiming to be born with an aversion to sunlight and a need for blood?

Disappointingly, true porphyriacs do not have lovely, ivory skin. In fact, according to medical journals and associated photography, their skin is rather damaged and blotchy-looking. Some serious cases lead the victim to have more of a mummified look than a vampiric one.

Someone with a more moderate case of porphyria would exhibit damaged skin and sharp teeth. Do you see where we're going with this? Depending on how hairy this individual is, he or she could be misconstrued as a wild animal-human hybrid in just the right lighting, or lack thereof. As a result, porphyria has been at times associated with werewolves in addition to vampires, making it an all-in-one condition for folklorists to mull over.

Personally, I can't see it being any more likely an explanation of all the werewolf legends than it is an explanation of vampirism. Not to get into population breakdowns after the Black Death, but extrapolating and doing a little math, there could have been as few as a hundred or so porphyriacs alive at any given time in the world while the legends were really hopping, as it were. Add to that the fact that the disease wasn't understood at all, and that many of them would have died young "without any reason" in broad daylight, and porphyria doesn't seem to be a winner as a lycanthropy explanation either.

Remember, the majority of werewolves were believed to be men and women who turned into actual wolves. Someone who always looked somewhat half-breed wouldn't have fit the description. And not a single person tried for the disease was recorded as looking anything but human in the revealing, daylight courtroom sessions.

Looks like it's time to say goodbye to porphyria in occult books.

ERGOTISM

The last medical explanation for lycanthropy is a combo explanation of sorts. That is, this one covers both the people who think they might be wolves and the people who think they see them everywhere. Ergotism is a unique form of poisoning caused by *Claviceps purpurea*, or ergot fungus. This sometimes difficult-to-detect fungus can grow on wheat and other crops, which can then end up tainting the majority of a village's food supply. Cooking it has no effect on its chemical nature. So all manner of raw and even prepared food could be a trip waiting to happen.

You've heard about mass hysteria. Ergotism is far, far worse.

The fungus causes two main types of problems that apply here. First, there's the physical discomfort. People suffering from ergotism could end up convulsing and feeling numb throughout their bodies. This can be accompanied by intense nausea and vomiting. Overall, the sensation in a superstitious society would be one of a body changing, or a body being under supernatural attack. All this would be accompanied by an intense feeling of mania. Literally a perfect combination to make one feel that something otherworldly is suddenly happening to one's body and soul.

The other main effect of ergotism is hallucinations, which can be intense and LSD-like. In fact, a derivative of ergot is LSD-25. Combined with the physical discomforts just described, these hallucinations would take on forms related to what the person is feeling. For example, if a person was doubled over on all fours from spasms, the hallucination could easily fill in the blanks for why he or she is in this position. The hallucinations could be external, too, making people see things moving around them that aren't really there.

In addition to seeing monsters, people suffering from ergotism could see ordinary people doing extraordinary things. Ergotism has been put forth as a possible explanation for much of the witch mania in the Middle Ages. Children would be put to bed by their maids, then hallucinate terrible things about these innocent women in the middle of the night, for example. The next morning often brought about horrible accusations from genuinely pained faces, and an arrest and death sentence for the maid whose only "crime" was being around after dinner.

Animals were subject to ergot poisoning as well. This may explain why livestock would also die as part of a family's "curse" from witches. Conspiracy theorists can rejoice that ergot poisoning wouldn't explain away cow mutilations, so those mysteries are still fair game.

Amazingly, ergotism is not only a disease from centuries ago. Depending on a region's sophistication and quality-assurance practices, local outbreaks are still possible. A Russian outbreak in 1926 affected some ten thousand victims. Another outbreak occurred in the French village of Pont-Saint-Esprit in 1951, with the hospital being so overwhelmed that private residences needed to be converted to wards to accommodate all the ill folks. Fifty years later still may have been the most recent outbreak: it's widely believed that in 2001, ergot-infected barley wreaked havoc in Ethiopia. Hallucinations accompanied all of these more recent outbreaks, although the cool eye of medicine didn't feel the need to report what the victims were seeing as being significant.

Some critics of the ergotism explanation for witchcraft and werewolf outbreaks suggest that people would have been able to recognize the signs of so-called Saint Anthony's Fire over time, and certainly by the time of the Salem witch trials in 1692. *Saint Anthony's Fire* was a name given to the disease in the twelfth century; however, scientific consistency was not so, well, consistent in the Middle Ages. It was difficult for people who had never experienced something to be able to diagnose it correctly.

Also, let's be blunt. While it may be that the scoundrels of the Inquisition would have been able to spot the signs of ergotism, the common man or woman wouldn't. Witchcraft trials were great for the booming business of organized religion. Being accused of sorcery pretty much guaranteed that you and maybe your family would be wiped out of existence. Where do you think all the seized land and property of these heretics ended up? It surely wasn't donated to the poor. So why would you bother to explain away certain supernatural attacks if the outcome was so economically rewarding? Dark times indeed.

An argument against ergotism is that infected food would have affected everyone in each house. This claim may be valid, but it's hard to say, centuries removed, how the effects would have varied. Keep in mind that even the Black Death, which is more potent, wasn't absolute. The plague wiped out half, not all, of Europe. People may have had resistance to ergotism, or at least just enough resistance to feel what must have been a typical occurrence: an upset stomach after dinner. This would be quickly forgotten while their neighbors were claiming to see werewolves running by at night.

CHAPTER NINE

NATIVE AMERICAN BELIEFS AND SHAMANISM

Most European werewolf legends seem to imply that actual physical transformations were taking place. Call it flawed reporting of the time period, but that's what people back then thought was happening. Flesh into furry flesh. To present a case that something other was taking place, we'll have to dig deep into the evidence that is hidden in plain sight, obscured by a lack of understanding from those who experienced the phenomena. Obscured, plain-sight clues can come together in compelling ways.

From here on out, this book will gradually shift focus to the clues that indicate werewolves might be something other than physical. We'll be going beyond the belief systems of those who thought werewolves were flesh-and-blood beings and explore how they may have been misled or fooled by their own senses.

While I'm all for letting my readers make up their own minds, I have to point out my personal opinion. After weighing all the evidence, and trying to mesh lycanthropy with the other hidden mysteries that we're understanding better with each passing scientific advancement (and occasional validation of an ancient theory), I can say with some confidence that if there is such a thing as a werewolf, it is not of the physical, fur-and-fang kind.

If we accept the notion that nonphysical werewolves are the only kinds of shapeshifters possible in the occult universe as we know it, can we point to a culture with a belief system that not only accepted such a possibility but also thoroughly integrated the possibility? In other words, was there a culture in which animal-human hybrids were an accepted part of the spiritual cosmology?

This book's opening vignette provides a dramatized glimpse of a Native American belief. Granted, in our tale the beast, physical or etheric, never got a chance to fully pass through the hut's fire hole (yet . . . you didn't skip to the conclusion, did you?). But which type of being did it seem like to you, with its surrounding howls? I left the description purposely vague for now, and not just for dramatic effect.

Shamanistic cultures from all around the world, including Native American cultures, fully blend worlds of spirit and the physical.

With their experience-earned, unique viewpoints, shamanistic cultures may have deep insight into why humankind became fascinated by a belief in the metamorphosis of humans into animal forms. This chapter will delve into those beliefs. First, we'll use the example of more varied Native American legends to start shifting this book's focus away from the physical and to what may be the most likely explanation for lycanthropy and all manner of shapeshifting.

TRIBES OF THE WOLF

Wolves, both natural and supernatural, permeate Native American cultures. It could be that their seeming group mind and orderly methods of hunting and surviving were admired by various tribes. Whatever the initial reason for it was, the introduction of wolf imagery, legends, and even names into Native American culture was impressive. Someone thinking of ancient China would find it hard not to see at least one stylized dragon in her mind's eye. The wolf would be just as apt when thinking of Native Americans.

Cherokee people held the wolf in high esteem, and no ordinary tribe member would kill one for fear of the wolf's pack seeking retribution. Only a specially trained member of the tribe's Wolf Clan could kill a wolf, either for ritual use of the parts or because a particular pack had become too threatening to the tribe's safety.

The Cheyenne had a legend about a tribe member who was near death and rescued by wolves that seemed to have mystical attributes. This tribe maintained a closeness with the animals, resulting in various folk beliefs. A wolf found asleep at dawn, for instance, was believed to be close to death. Also, hunters in the tribe would rub wolf fur on arrows before hunting to ensure good luck.

Sioux tribes believed that wolves were really spirits in a doglike form. Considering how Christmas appears in so many werewolf tales from Europe, it's interesting that the Sioux thought of the December full moon as the "Moon When the Wolves Run Together."

Another stellar connection to wolves was found in the Pawnee tribe, who considered the star we call Sirius to be the Wolf Star (we call it the Dog Star in astronomy, so not a big stretch). The Wolf Star ran along the Milky Way, which was called the Wolf Road, and its movement suggested that a great wolf spirit was coming and going from the underworld as the star rose and settled in the night sky. Other tribes called the Pawnee "wolves," because of their hunting prowess and ability to prowl like the creatures and make long journeys.

In recent years, a particular tribe of Native Americans has grown in notoriety thanks to Stephenie Meyer's *Twilight* series of novels, and the accompanying movies. While she took a few liberties with her tale, adding "cold ones" to introduce her vampires to the mythology, Meyer did base a good amount of her fictional Quileutes on the real Quileute (sometimes spelled *Quillayute*) tribe.

WILL THE REAL QUILEUTES PLEASE SHAPESHIFT?

Because of the popularity of *Twilight*, and how it's replaced Anne Rice's *Vampire Chronicles* for a new generation of vampire fans, an increasing number of questions I've received come from those who want to know if there is any truth to Meyer's vampires. To such curious folks, I say: what I wrote in *Vampires: The Occult Truth* still applies. I don't think you'll be running into an Edward any time soon, ladies. Surprisingly, this doesn't mean Meyer's Native American tribe of werewolves is a fabrication.

The Quileute are a real tribe, still living in the Pacific Northwest on a reservation they secured with a treaty in 1855 (yes, it's called La Push in modern times). While their numbers are depleted—a recent unofficial count numbers them at about 750—some of their most fantastic legends survive among the people. They have their own tribal council and businesses open to the public, including a resort. Oh yeah, and they really claim to be descended from wolves!

According to the most ancient legends of the people, the Quileute tribe was formed when a traveling mystic, a shapeshifter, came across a wolf while wandering through what would become the tribe's lands. This shapeshifter transformed the wolf into a man, creating the first

Quileute. Because of his ability to change the shape of another, the mystic has been called the Transformer. The knowledge of how many wolves this Transformer was supposed to have turned into men and women is lost to time, but the tribe was born.

Despite their legend of descending from wolves, the tribe was not tied to a particular animal spirit in its mystical pursuits. As with many other Native American cultures, a rite of passage involved having a young boy go on a vision quest in search of his own personal totem. The Quileute called this animal spirit a *taxilit*. Once they discovered the identity of this spirit, the Quileute would pray to both it and the greater universal spirit, or *Tsikáti*. The taxilit of many boys would have likely been a wolf, because of its importance in their creation legend, but it's just as likely that the spirit could have been a salmon, since an important ritual of the tribe is designed to coax the help of salmon spirits in having scores of the fish fill the nets of the Quileute.

Unlike in the *Twilight* stories, there is no prevailing belief that the Quileute boys will turn back into wolves at any point in time, nor is there an ages-old war with vampires. Supernatural creatures such as the *Duskiya*, a "kelp-haired child snatcher," exist in the lore, and legend obviously implies that shapeshifters like the Transformer are out there, but werewolves are not found in their woods these days, it seems.

Tribes located nearby in the Pacific Northwest practiced bizarre wolf rituals, something that is certainly worth mentioning here. The Nootka, for example, had a belief that long ago a young man was stolen by wolves and befriended by them. They sent the man back to his people to teach the others wolf rites that would grant them powers from the wolves. The ritual attributed to this legend was typically performed before the full moon at the start of winter (again, Christmastime enters a wolf legend). It sounded like quite a psychodramatic ritual, too, as it was designed to simulate a kidnapping by wolves.

The wolves of the ritual were tribal elders wearing wolf masks made of real wolf skins. The chosen participant of the ritual was taken by the wolf men and put through various ordeals; such a concept of suffering or proverbial passing through the fire was common to the initiatory rituals of most cultures. At the end of the ordeals, the changed individual was allowed to come back to the tribe. After this initiation, the participant was supposed to possess new, wolflike powers.

Similar rituals may have been practiced at one point by the Quileute, considering the latter's origin tale and close proximity to the Nootka. Even if the Quileute did practice the ritual, it is still not a technique designed to shapeshift, of course. But it's a colorful form of initiation that helps cement the importance of the Pacific Northwest tribes in the lore of werewolves.

NAVAJO WEREWOLVES AND ANIMAL MYSTERIES

It's common knowledge that Christopher Columbus was not the first European to set foot in the "New World." Roughly five hundred years before the man of October honor landed in the West Indies, a Viking named Leif Ericson landed much closer to North America proper. Archaeology seems to indicate that Ericson made a settlement in Newfoundland just after 1000 CE, calling the discovered region Vinland. No one knows the extent of the cultural impact these Vikings might have had on any Native Americans who either lived nearby or happened upon the foreign settlement. Is it possible that they carried across the sea and transmitted, from the land of the berserkers, the belief in animal-human hybrids and shapeshifting?

While any assimilation of European folklore into Native American tribes is difficult to trace, it seems as if select tribes from around North America developed similar beliefs independently. A perfect example is the Navajo, centered in what is now the American Southwest. To the Navajo, certain animal-based legends are so organic a part of their belief system that it seems impossible to imagine their culture without these ideas fully integrated.

A Tricky, Talented Coyote

Navajo mythology contains an anthropomorphic coyote god, referred to in translations as a proper noun: Coyote. In his most lighthearted tales, Coyote is a trickster and always up to mischief. Shamanistic cultures always seem to have a trickster god, almost as if it serves some need for balancing humor with serious pursuits like the occult. In darker beliefs attributed to him, Coyote is tied to evil "witchcraft." So important was this upright walking dog of sorts that he is tied to the Navajo's creation myths, performing actions so archetypal and part of the collective unconscious that they have appeared in other cultures' early myths. For example, Coyote caused a great flood in one myth.

Coyote is also tied to death. His physical spawn—real-world running, howling coyotes—have been viewed with superstitious fear by the Navajo as a result. Depending on the era of religious development in the tribe, seeing a coyote or having it cross your path either meant an omen of death, or that you were viewing an evil person returned from the underworld in the canine form.

Perhaps the most interesting attribute of Coyote is his ability to shapeshift. This mythological power of his, combined with his already half-man look (remember, he walked upright), led to some natural connections in the minds of the Navajo. Some Navajo believe that painting one's face like Coyote could allow for a shift into a werecreature, though not necessarily a werecoyote. Curiously, the Navajo did not spread many legends of werecoyotes. Their creatures of the night were still werewolves proper.

Hogan-Haunting Werewolves

When dealing with a culture that has been around long enough to have its belief systems passed down orally, you begin to expect that legends will morph and combine, or get a whole lot better, over time. The Navajo belief in werewolves has definitely been subjected to this. We can no longer clearly identify about when the first belief in werewolves appeared in the tribe, and we can't hope to separate the more phantomlike beliefs from the ones that seem to indicate fur-and-bone beings. With that said, the beliefs overall do point more to the idea of spiritual, rather than physical, lycanthropy.

The opening anecdote of this book is a dramatized example of what a scared child in a Navajo village could have believed was crawling on top of his hogan or hut. In her excellent 1945 book on Navajo beliefs called *Spin a Silver Dollar*, Alberta Hannum shares some other clues that seem to indicate the werewolf may be a spiritual one:

> *Sometimes the wolf would knock four times, or sometimes the people inside the hogan would only hear the mud falling from the roof and know it was the wolf there. But always, with or without warning, the wolf appeared with paralyzing slowness to its victims—peeping around the corner of the door blanket, or letting just its eyes show for a while over the hole in the roof, and then slowly the rest of him.*[1]

No matter the size of the fire hole in the roof it's on top of, the werewolf can always somehow get through, and does so gracefully in description after description. There would be nothing agonizingly slow about an 80-pound non-supernatural wolf coming down through a hole it managed to fit through, and few werewolves have ever been described as being the same size as an ordinary wolf.

Obviously, real wolves differ from the aforementioned description in ways other than their not being able to defy gravity and passageway-sized constraints. Real wolves typically don't knock, let alone knock four times. Also, a great many of these beliefs contain a sleeping witness who wakes up either from the noise or merely by sensing that something sinister is approaching. Folklore is full of experiences that involve waking up in the middle of the night, sensing that something "other" is nearby, and then being unable to move as this thing makes it way toward the victim. In *Vampires: The Occult Truth*, I talk about the hag attack, and the belief that the dark figure coming to the victim is either a "witch" out of body, or an evil individual continuing to draw energy from the living long after the sorcerer has died—a form of psychic vampirism.

The attacks during which something other is sensed in the room at night are not always of a draining nature. Sometimes they just feature a feeling of terror; sometimes they're so violent as to be hard for skeptics to take seriously, complete with victims being scratched and tossed about the room. Can phantom werewolf experiences be yet another cultural interpretation of the hag attack or night-visitor phenomenon? After all, one can argue that in modern, sci-fi-friendly times, the alien abduction experience is little more than our minds dressing up the same sensation of being visited.

The idea that Navajo werewolves could be sorcerers visiting enemies in astral form is not exactly unprecedented. The culture intimately associates werewolves with sorcery. Changing into an animal to get to a witches' meeting was believed to be standard operating procedure for the supernatural beings living in a tribe. These witches were called *yee naaldlooshii*, and their practice was similar to some of the voluntary werewolves of Europe. The sorcerer would wear the animal's skin in a ritual, which is where the phrase *yee naaldlooshii* comes from, as it means "those who trot about with it," meaning the animal skin. For this reason, the sorcerers were also called *skinwalkers* (a general term that is not exclusive to the Navajo). If a typical superstitious tribe member entered someone's hut and saw a coyote or wolf skin lying there, the first conclusion he or she would draw is that the owner of the hut was a skinwalker or witch capable of shapeshifting. Never mind the lack of a clothing store for the Navajo to go pick up something else to wear during the cold months—having an animal skin was proof enough!

So, with all these elements introduced, can we conclude whether the Navajo believe this shapeshifting to be spiritual or physical? Adding extra weight to the idea that the werewolves had no weight at all is the belief that Navajo skinwalkers could move at unnatural speeds on the way to their meetings. William Morgan, an anthropologist who interviewed the Navajo in the 1930s, was told that a skinwalker could cover the same distance in an hour and a half that a then-current car could travel in four hours. This certainly seems to mesh nicely with the sensation most commonly reported by those who have an out-of-body experience: the rush of moving almost instantaneously to a destination or back into one's body.

Again, it's easier to accept an occult belief if it plays nicely with other beliefs.

A strange encounter from 1970 seems to bear out the high-speed type of lycanthrope. Four young adults driving in New Mexico were startled to find that a wolflike creature running on two legs was easily keeping up with their car, even at a speed of sixty miles per hour. One of the group was a violent type, apparently, as he pulled out a gun and shot the mysterious creature. They stopped and watched the beast fall as if the bullet affected it. But this didn't turn out to be the case. The creature quickly got up, and they were able to see that it didn't have any blood on it. It then ran off in a different direction just as quickly as before.

Deadly Arts

Navajo werewolves have a more sinister connection to sorcery than just using it to travel in wolf form. A common belief is that they could create a magical potion or powder that could cause tuberculosis. The werewolf could deliver this powder to its victims in a number of ways, including pouring it on them or adding it to their hogan's fire. This powder was made from a variety of ingredients over the years, including a man's finger and a young girl's tongue. Why a werewolf would opt for such a slow death rather than making a meal of the victim is unclear. Another parallel to vampirism comes in with this disease-based legend. Tuberculosis, and its associated death by wasting, was often explained away as someone dying over time from a vampire's repeated attacks.

Still another Navajo werewolf belief explains why a sorcerer may have been able to get the gruesome ingredients for the tuberculosis-causing powder. The skinwalkers were thought to dig up the graves of the dead to steal their jewels. Perhaps they removed a finger or tongue in the process? No matter what they did when they got there, such literally ghoulish behavior is not found in other lycanthropic belief systems. Werewolves usually are content to put animals and humans into their graves and be done with them at that point.

The ghoulish belief did not vanish hundreds of years ago, either. As recently as 1946 in Arizona, the Navajo believed that one of their own was exactly such a grave-robbing werewolf. A well-rounded beast, he also indulged in the usual mauling of animals and tribe members. He was sighted on at least one occasion still in human form, running in a wolf skin, supposedly before he transformed, although no one saw the actual change into wolf happen. The suspect's home did contain a large amount of silver jewelry believed to be taken from the various graves. This may prove the grave-robbing part of his alleged crimes, at least, but nothing tied him to the murders going on in the village.

Even though I'm strongly leaning toward the possibility that all lycanthropy can be explained by some kind of visionary experience or actual out-of-body travel, elements of legend still complicate that. Finding stolen jewelry is one such problem, unless the evil magician did his robbing in human form. A further possibility is that an astral body can affect the material world.

I'll have lots more to say in the following two chapters in support of the idea that werewolves are either people experiencing purely internal experiences, or people or other beings that are interacting with the world in a very real but etheric way.

A MODERN NATIVE AMERICAN EXPERIENCE

Before we start to pile on the evidence for the more mystical types of werewolves, I have to include a recent experience from a Native American that I found interesting. This is the last bit of evidence in the book to support the possibility that a werewolf could simply be imagining his or her state of being, and then acting physically in tandem, much like someone with medical lycanthropy "showing" a transformation in a psychiatric ward. Not to say the person observed in the following eyewitness account was a typical clinical case. This may reveal what a strong cultural background can do to skew inner feelings.

This is not a fur-and-fang type of werewolf experience, so there's no need to put great emphasis in whether it is true or not. I can't vouch for its authenticity, but I can say that the associated messages that accompanied it do not fall into what I can affectionately call the "out there" camp. The event related in the following e-mail really could have happened to someone who got carried away with deep-seated cultural beliefs:

> Being Native American, I was always taught in my family that shape-shifting is a possibility. This was so common that I remember how others in my tribe would even excuse some people's disappearances, saying that they had shifted and then gone away. I never really believed it, though, till I saw something with my own eyes.
>
> Through high school we had a strange friend, which is the best thing I can call him. So let's call him SF [strange friend] in my letter if

you use it. Everyone had weird things to say about him, and he helped this along by claiming to be "another being." I basically thought he was full of shit. I'd have to see something with my own eyes to believe it, Konstantinos.

Well, one summer night SF proved . . . something. And it still chills me to this day, what I saw. I've never told anyone because I didn't think anyone outside my tribe would believe me. I don't remember if there was a full moon or not, and don't know what triggered this friend's change.

A small group of us was outside in a wooded area at about 2 a.m. We were walking along a trail and SF was in front of us. He started making these strange movements, flinging his arms around. Then he started growling. He got down on all fours with his back extremely arched, and he began clawing violently at the ground. In seconds his fingers became ragged, and I could see lots of blood even in the dim light.

We all had stopped dead in our tracks and just watched. We didn't know whether to run or help him, and we were all scared.

SF stood back up and his body was so twisted. His arms looked out of their sockets, and he was shaking uncontrollably. He acted like he was in terrible pain. Somehow, he looked taller than usual. He turned around and looked at us standing there. I swear his eyes were shining in the dark. I can't even describe the freaky noises coming from his mouth at this point. He was salivating madly.

Then he ran off suddenly. None of us ever saw him again. Although, we did hear a rumor that he ended up killing a family member wherever he disappeared to. I was never able to prove the rumor that the murder actually happened.

If the above is true, this reader has witnessed something less dramatic than a horror movie, but something dramatic enough to have affected superstitious individuals if it happened hundreds of years ago. Imagine coming across someone in such throes in the woods at night in a prescientific world.

SHAMANS BLEND THE WORLDS

A chapter on Native American beliefs this may be, but shamanism is an occult practice that is common to cultures around the world. The most basic tenet of the pursuit is that the shaman can act as an intermediary between the physical plane of existence and the spirit world. People in a village either visit a shaman looking for supernatural help with specific problems, or the shaman uses his or her abilities without prompting. Either way, the end result is the same. By traveling to a spiritual realm that exists either within or without the shaman, he or she can accomplish amazing, tangible feats that manifest somehow in the physical world. For all its critics, shamanism is as prevalent around the world as is the belief in gods.

The most common reason people visit a shaman is to obtain some kind of healing. Not surprisingly, basic needs like health and well-being come first. If someone is ill and there is no access to traditional medicine, some cultures believe that a shaman can go on a vision quest and defeat some malevolent force that is causing the illness, or bring back some type of intangible medicine that can be mystically applied to help. It could be power of suggestion and placebo for the believer being healed, but the general consensus around the world is that these healings often work.

The other main reason people rely on shamans is for answers to some difficult question or problem. This is also the reason a shaman most often goes on vision quests for himself or herself—to obtain a type of wisdom from the internal or spirit world, although for a true ascetic shaman the wisdom sought after will usually be of a type that can advance the shaman spiritually and not materialistically.

So, what does all this have to do with werewolves? For starters, shamans often take on the form of their spirit animals or totems when they venture into the inner realms. From the perspective of the shaman, this is a very real shapeshifting experience. They fully assume this animal form, begin their journey, accomplish something miraculous, then revert back to both normal human shape and consciousness. An uninitiated outsider hearing about this "transformation," possibly through translation, could easily misinterpret what he or she is being told was happening. But we don't need to speculate as to whether an error in translation led to the start of shapeshifting beliefs. The beliefs of the shaman and their associated reality stand on their own for those who have experienced them. This idea that a person has a spiritual animal nature is adhered to by some modern individuals who are not necessarily animals. They call themselves *therianthropes* (literally, "beast people"), and don't necessarily believe they can turn into their totem, or animal with which they most closely identify. The term has lost its original use and meaning. It used to be that *therianthrope* was a more generic shapeshifting term, reserved to describe physically transforming werecreatures that were not specifically lycanthropes or werewolves. More on modern therianthropes in the final chapter.

Another interesting parallel to shapeshifting found in shamanism is the idea that perhaps human eyewitnesses to werewolves and other mystical creatures were beholding otherdimensional beings and not necessarily ones that are transformed humans. The beings that shamans encounter while on their vision quests do seem to have some type of archetypal and independent reality, and are of an exotic-animal or even animal-human form.

Much more on this in the next chapter, when we examine how people without an upbringing in shamanistic cultures still encounter the same, seemingly independent beings when helped into such a trance without any training!

SIMULATED TRANSFORMATIONS

What benefits would hunters obtain from trying to assimilate properties of wolves and other animals? Recall that the berserkers and Úlfhednar would wear animal pelts to enter their battle rages. It is certainly possible that some of these ideas may have either been explained to one or more Native American tribes around 1000 CE, or that some of these tribe members witnessed such a ritual one night by firelight and drew their own conclusions. Misunderstanding is the mother of most legends, after all.

However, it is just as likely that the hunters who wanted the "powers" of certain animals took a more shamanistic approach to obtaining them.

Hunters were typically not mystics in Native American culture. Still, they were surrounded by a culture that embraced certain mysteries. Believing that you could gain even brief access into the unseen world on at least some level would have seemed as natural to hunters of such a culture as tapping into the unseen world of wireless communications networks seems to non-techies who use cell phones. Even if you don't really understand a "technology" or energy, and can't fully get under the hood to take control of it, you can at least try to tap into it as a user.

Hunters would have known that shamans take on animal forms on their vision quests and then accomplish great things while in those forms. That would have been the marvel of the day worth trying out. With a simple like-attracts-like philosophy, the hunters would have tried getting excited for a big kill by emulating a predator they admired, perhaps by dancing around a fire in its pelt and making the noises it is known for. After such psychodrama, it is likely they would be more in tune with their reflexes and hunting senses before heading out. Everything might indeed work more in sync in the hunter's body afterward.

Not true shapeshifting, but truly a changing experience, even if a temporary one.

CHAPTER TEN

OTHERDIMENSIONAL BEINGS

As ancient as some Native American beliefs and practices may seem in the modern world, they hardly date back to the earliest days of *Homo sapiens*. Consider that even the oldest of the so-called "early man" archaeological sites seem to indicate that America was barren of humans over 13,000 years ago. A famous cave in France, the Grotte Chauvet, makes that time period seem almost recent. The French site has cave paintings believed to be 32,000 years old! And what are these cave paintings of?

Animal-human hybrids, you guessed?

While we build some pseudo-suspense on the answer for a moment, let's first establish where we're going with this chapter's main argument. Put simply, human consciousness experienced some kind of change virtually overnight. We can't be sure exactly when it occurred, but somewhere in the time period between 50,000 and 32,000 years ago, some type of early visionary experience had a permanent impact. The resulting shift in consciousness may have shaped the course of the world's first religions and supernatural beliefs. What brought about this change in consciousness and the early belief in animal-human hybrids? Was it an actual encounter of some kind? If so, we need to consider whether this encounter took place "here" in the physical world.

The answers to the aforementioned questions may be found in this chapter, as we explore our third type of werewolf: the otherdimensional being. Technically, beings like this do not fit the traditional definition of the word *werewolf*. Otherdimensional beings are full-time supernatural entities that humans have encountered, rather than physical beings that transform into wolflike creatures after having been human. Semantics would let you argue that because of its sometimes anthropomorphic appearance, an otherdimensional being can be a permanently blended "man-wolf" or some other type of man- or woman-creature. Playing around with words and meanings is not all that important when you're searching for explanations of the supernatural, however. If this type of being would explain a lot of werewolf sightings and beliefs, granting it werewolf status doesn't seem like such a stretch.

THE FIRST SIGHTINGS

Back to the caves. What prompted Paleolithic humans living 32,000 years ago to paint animal-human hybrids on the walls of their caves? The most recent archaeological theories indicate that the figures were revered. These images weren't meant to be early attempts at entertainment or shock art—these were representations of beings that the early painters had either met and were awed by, or met and wanted to be like. Notice the repeated use of the word *met*. The prevailing opinion is that these creatures were drawn to re-create what the painters believed was reality.

The figures vary greatly. One, which is called the "sorcerer" in the academic field, is part man, part bison. Another features a human top and more of a seal-like bottom. The variety of hybrid-being images, combined with the types of scenes they're a part of, implies that the paintings might be depictions of shamanistic journeys taken in the form of different spirit totems, or journeys to meet different animal-human hybrids on the inner realms.

One thing we may never be able to sort out is which of the images are drawings of visions, wishes, and actual transformations of some type. Some of the images clearly depict something the ancients saw in a vision. But it is possible that some of the hybrid drawings were made up by the ancients to show what they wished they could do. It is equally possible that some of the transformations they painted are re-creations of a transformation the painters believe they underwent, perhaps in a vision quest where they assumed an animal form. Ultimately, this is a distinction I can live without.

We can fault the ancients for not differentiating their cave pictures with captions. The fact that they likely met otherdimensional beings in a trance is exciting enough. We don't need to know if 100 percent of their drawings were re-creations of the beings, as long as 100 percent of them were inspired in some way by meeting the beings. Again, the introduction of these beings into the ancients' lives was a consciousness-changing event.

A logical question to ask is how did the earliest of shamans learn how to make contact with these previously unseen worlds and beings? The universe didn't exactly provide a manual for such undertakings.

Unlike herbalism, which can be learned through inference and trial and error, shamanism is just not observable in nature. Early humans could observe someone accidentally eat an herb and then note how they feel afterward. Perhaps a certain pain went away as a result, or some other verifiable effect. Yet our early ancestors couldn't just observe someone eat an herb and enter a trance.

No, wait. They could do exactly that!

ENTHEOGENS

Anthropology can't ignore how there literally was no knowledge of spiritual beings one "day" (i.e., time period), and then instantaneously a rich plethora of animal-human hybrid entities appeared in cave paintings. It's puzzling if you approach such a mystery with a closed mind, but dare I say the solution becomes obvious if you expand your mind to the realm of mind expansion.

Some of the most impressive solutions to this puzzle come from a neuropsychological rather than an archaeological model. Neuropsychology in this context involves studying the types of images depicted in the French cave art, as well as those found on artifacts from other regions. With enough images to work with, we can determine a pattern in the types of imagery shown. The pattern is apparent. These rendered worlds are always lush, and contain bizarre geometric patterns. Inhabiting these abstract panoramas are, of course, the animal-human hybrids, drawn in a way that indicates their great importance amidst the backgrounds.

These specific, expected images can be counted on to appear in certain types of art, ancient and new. We see the art elements repeatedly at what can be considered the start of religion. And we see them when even modern individuals take a type of hallucinogenic known as an *entheogen*—literally something that creates God, or causes God to be, within an individual. These substances may account for everything from the aforementioned cave paintings to the animal-headed gods of Egypt.

One of the biggest supporters of the idea that entheogens may have been the inspiration for the seeming shift that took place in consciousness in the Paleolithic era is David Lewis-Williams, a professor emeritus of cognitive archaeology at the University of the Witwatersrand in Johannesburg. His work focuses primarily on San rock art in southern Africa and the rituals of the San people, but the universal parallels are still there: people all tend to see similar things while in a trance state that is induced by an entheogen. This shared type of experience is also available to individuals who learn how to closely mimic the trance state through techniques such as drumming and deep meditation. Not all or even most shamans need the help of substances.

Thanks to popular culture, the best-known entheogen is a peculiar small cactus called peyote. Almost as if nature intended for us to take a bite out of the little "buttons" growing on it, the plant does not have the usual intimidating needles found on other cacti. The buttons contain a drug called mescaline, which has been used for millennia to alter consciousness. Combined with any kind of ritualistic setting, the effects of mescaline can be made more extreme and focused on a specific theme. However it's taken, mescaline provides visions that can last for half a day. In its raw form, the drug has been known to be hard to stomach, and many would-be shamans make a trip to a bathroom or the bushes to vomit long before they give their circulatory and nervous systems a chance to propel their consciousness into a visionary trip.

Another ready-to-go hallucinogenic plant is iboga, or ibogaine, which contains everything needed to ingest it effectively. In addition to inducing spiritual visions, this plant has an interesting side effect of curing addictions to dangerous substances like heroin. Not to get political, but ibogaine is a drug whose legal status governments should reconsider. Ibogaine can cure addictions by changing how the pleasure centers of the brain operate, acting on serotonin and opiate systems. In addition to slowing down a person's craving for dangerous drugs, ibogaine can also take the edge off someone's withdrawal symptoms. Despite its beneficial applications and how it exists in nature in a form that needs minimal preparation to act as a hallucinogen, ibogaine is not the most well-known of the entheogens. That honor, if I can use that word, goes to a potion with an active ingredient that has been studied as recently as 1990 in a university-hosted scientific setting.

The ayahuasca potion is a bitter drink that, like the aforementioned substances, can cause nausea and vomiting in those who aren't used to it (and in more than a few who are used to it!). Made from a mixture of plant parts, ayahuasca is the most natural way to introduce extra amounts of dimethyltryptamine (DMT) into the bloodstream. That's right, the potion contains a drug that is already present in the human body. Getting the extra DMT into the bloodstream orally requires bypassing the effects of an enzyme in our digestive tracts known as *monoamine oxidase*, or MAO. Ordinarily, MAO is helpful, preventing the excessive flow of neurotransmitters in our nervous system. Due to its chemical nature, though, MAO also prevents tryptamines like DMT from working when taken orally. The ayahuasca potion contains an MAO inhibitor to allow DMT to work its magic.

Taking DMT is a powerful experience, as it launches its users instantly into other, more ultra-realistic realms—the realms of the cave paintings. The trip usually only lasts a few minutes, but there can be hallucinatory experiences for a day or two afterward. What you see on such a trip comes seemingly from elsewhere, and almost always appears to be from something higher, complete with the feeling of flying up to meet greater powers.

The rich visuals of a DMT trip have to be experienced to be believed. Including bizarre geometric shapes and vivid colors, and having an overall sensation of overlapping realities, this trip still manages to avoid feeling like chaos. Somehow it all makes sense and seems real. It feels more like stepping into an amusement park you heard about as a child, but totally forgot existed, than stepping into a theater to watch an experimental film.

Back to how this connects with the belief in animal-human hybrids. Most people who experience an entheogenic trip even once claim that they are not alone when they arrive. For some travelers it takes a couple of times to meet them, but the others appear. They are always somewhere in the colorful landscape if you seek them out. These others are humanoid, but always have something animal blended in, ranging from insectoid to furry. The more insectoid faces have been called alien-looking by some, while the furry ones have resembled all manner of hybrids, including our modern, anthropomorphic, movie-type werewolves.

These beings occasionally remain quiet, but sometimes have wisdom to share, which is why shamans seek them out in their vision quests. Because they seem to exist in a more amazing realm than our physical world, they instantly demand respect. A modern traveler to such a realm can see why the beings would have been thought of as role models of a type by our ancestors. It is not a stretch to imagine that the first travelers to these realms would have wanted to aspire to emulate and be more like the hybrid beings. Such a longing alone can account for the first tales of humans shapeshifting into animals of all types, wolves included.

According to the ancients and even to modern shamans, these types of experiences seem real because they are real—because they take one to very real places. Most modern scientists couldn't possibly entertain the idea that these realms are actual dimensions, could they?

MODERN RESEARCH INTO TUNING IN

The question of whether visionary experiences actually let us tune in to other dimensions is one that literally *had to be* pondered during a series of DMT experiments conducted at the University of New Mexico's School of Medicine in Albuquerque. The ramifications—the possibility that our minds can work like radio receivers with DMT-modified antennas, tuning in to what is normally out of reach for our senses—are astounding. This alternate-dimension idea was not a hypothesis that Dr. Rick Strassman, associate professor of psychiatry, set out to prove in 1990, which makes it even more amazing. The idea grew organically during research, as have all great advancements in science.

Dr. Strassman had some hurdles to overcome to conduct his research. As you can imagine, asking even the university where you're tenured for the right to give patients a controlled drug is not without legal hurdles and enough red tape to turn a snow peak into a giant peppermint candy! Perseverance paid off, though, and Dr. Strassman was able to inject sixty volunteers with approximately four hundred doses of DMT over the course of five years of experiments.

The injection method was less nauseating than drinking ayahuasca and even smoking DMT (which is another way to bypass the MAO found in the body). Overall, the participants were able to tolerate the drug well via injection, and reported on some of the most amazing experiences ever recorded in a university experiment. Dr. Strassman detailed the experiences and his conclusions regarding his research in his excellent 2001 book, *DMT: The Spirit Molecule*.

At least half of Dr. Strassman's test subjects were able to make contact with otherdimensional beings. They described them as everything from entities to aliens. While some of them looked unusual in unexpected ways, such as clowns or stick figures, a good number were reptiles, mantises, bees, spiders, and other animals.

If these experiences have some subjective reality, we have to wonder if the hybrid beings encountered can be seen by humans who are not fully in a trance state, but who have only slightly slipped in their state into something like a daydream. This could explain a large number of phenomena, such an ability to accidentally witness the other realms. And if they're filled with animal-human hybrids, then it could explain quite a bit indeed in our current subject matter. People could be occasionally slipping into altered states and reporting things like the Beast of Bray Road.

If these beings are real, we have to consider how important their existence will eventually prove to be. As Dr. Strassman puts it:

> . . . we are pressed far beyond our comfort zone as clinician-researchers when dealing with psychedelic subjects who return telling tales of contact and interactions with seemingly autonomous nonmaterial entities. How, then, do we study these "transdimensional" properties of DMT?
>
> We must begin by assuming that these types of experiences are "possibly real." In other words, they may indicate "what it's like" in alternate realities. The earliest attempts at systematically investigating these contacts should determine the consistency and stability of the beings. With lessening shock at their presence, is it possible to prolong, expand, and deepen our interactions with them?[1]

The longer our interactions with such beings can be, the better chance we have at validating information they provide. A good question to ask is simply: are you the reason people have been seeing werewolves?

For such a thing to be possible as an explanation, we really need to know whether contact with these beings and their realms can be made without entheogens.

Recall that DMT is present in small amounts in the human body. Some have theorized that it is stored in the pineal gland and is released at certain moments, resulting in strong visions—such as during a near-death experience (NDE). That is purely involuntary, of course. Most people don't seem to have the ability to release DMT on demand.

A rule of thumb in the entheogenic scene is that about 2 percent of individuals can release DMT at will into their bloodstream, and that these individuals can have full visionary experiences without ever taking the drug. This low percentage matches up well with how few shamans were present in each village of relevant cultures. But it is likely that almost everyone can release at least trace amounts of it without willing it to happen. Again, NDEs are not voluntary experiences, and perhaps encountering an otherdimensional "werewolf" is not voluntary either.

I KIND OF ASKED FOR THIS

When I wrote my book *Nocturnicon*, I introduced the idea of using entheogens in combination with ritual. While the long-standing view of occultists who play it safe has always been to avoid substances, I challenged this notion as being too politically correct to make psychodramatic sense. Think about it. If ritual is psychodrama designed to bring about a change in consciousness, then why not start such a ritual more than halfway there?

Not surprisingly, some readers took it upon themselves to consult their local laws (I hope), and to attempt using what is for them legal entheogenic substances (I can still hope) to lift the veil between the worlds.

So let me reiterate: Do not break any laws while doing your very best to get to a psychodramatic state. Read that as you will.

The title of the subhead above has a double meaning. Sure, by talking about entheogens in a book I was unintentionally inviting readers to share experiences they'd had with them—say, during a trip to a jungle to partake in ayahuasca. So I did ask for that.

This subhead title also appears in one of the most amazing e-mails I've ever received from a reader. I'll even forgive his incredibly transparent attempt at disguising which entheogen he took to have the experience he shares here:

I'll spare you the knowledge of what I took that night, Mr. Konstantinos. If you decide to use this e-mail in a sequel to Nocturnicon or some other book, just call me Jason and forget about the three capital letters I wrote in the subject line. [awesome save, Jason!]

It came on as fast as all the books said it would. I guess I didn't believe it would because I was standing in front of a wicker chair when I took my only hit, and when it was over I found myself way in the chair. Butt through the chair. It's okay, I hated that crappy old chair anyway.

The trip. I didn't move through my living room like an out-of-body experience or anything. My room was just gone. Even with the insane pull upwards I felt I knew my room was gone.

The colors around me as I moved up changed too fast for me to identify what they were. Does that make sense? I could see each color, but couldn't commit it to memory fast enough. Maybe that's why some people think they are seeing colors that don't exist while they are in dreams or on a trip. Shrug.

In what felt like the fastest year or longest 10 seconds I arrived down. I know I said I rose up, but the feeling I had was of landing with my feet while moving up. I was inside a transparent pyramid that had dozens of sides and still looked like a pyramid. At least that's what I first thought I saw around me. On closer inspection the shape revealed itself to be a series of bent triangles moving through each other. Double shrug here. They all looked bent out of shape yet still met at the corners.

While I was looking through one of these triangles, I saw him for the first time. As each open area of the triangle moved in a slow turn to pass through empty, glowing "color space" it let me catch a glimpse of his hunched-over form.

There was nothing human about this thing. I could tell that—even though the moving shapes didn't sit still long enough for me to see all of him at once. I reached out and grabbed on to one to hold it still, and it turned into a glowing circle. I caught a glimpse of my hand and felt as if I was about to lose the vision, so I looked into the circle instead.

He was there. All of him. Mega shrug. I have no idea what he was. He was covered in something that looked like hair and mud mixed together. His stomach was the only part that didn't look like it was covered with this mud hair. It was blue. Not glowing, just blue, like bright paint on a human stomach.

I was afraid to focus on his face. I had a clear thought. I didn't know if it would be worse to find him looking at me with intelligence or hunger. A weird thought, right? When I remembered this thought after, there was no question. Awake I'm pretty sure I would pick intelligence!

Then I bit the bullet and looked up at his face. This would be the end of the trip, and it was also the most startling part. His face zoomed in as if the circle was an eyepiece to an even bigger telescope. It felt like a split second, and his giant, hairy face moved 100 yards until it was almost touching me. I couldn't smell him or feel his breath. It was purely visual. And what I saw wasn't human at all. I want to say it reminded me of Anubis because its snout was so long, and it was kind of dark, but it wasn't black and the hair must have been fur. I could see that it was fur now.

This thing was some kind of wolf with one mother of a long snout!

I'm so glad it didn't open that mouth. If I had seen those teeth I think I would have voided my bowels as people drinking ayahuasca in the jungle are said to sometimes do!

When the trip ended I would have jumped up out of the chair I was so wired, but I was stuck in that chair like I said. After a few minutes of wriggling out and making sure there were no splinters sticking out of my lower regions I was free to freak out.

I kind of asked for this. But after having read some other people's experiences with beings like this, I think I've got my Irish up again. I'm planning on asking for it again.

I urged Jason to reach out to Dr. Strassman in case he gets approval to begin another round of experimentation. Sounds like they'd hit it off.

For the record, Jason had no idea I was writing a book on werewolves when he sent this e-mail. I know this because I didn't either at the time. But I wonder if Jason knows a peculiar tidbit about the god Anubis, the minor deity that Jason thought for a moment the being might be. In really ancient Egypt, before what people usually think of as ancient Egypt (to keep things simple), there was a god named Wepwawet, who was a sort of wolf-headed god of war. The region where he was worshiped was called Atef-Khen, or Lycopolis by the Greeks. It may be that he was later morphed into a different role in the form of jackal-headed Anubis. Not that I'm implying it was an Egyptian deity in Jason's vision, but it's an interesting link to point out. Recall that Egypt came up earlier in this chapter. Anthropologists studying the entheogenic phenomenon have looked to Egypt as a possible place where religion could have been inspired by visions. The only issue with the theory is it's hard to prove which substance would have been the entheogen responsible.

Maybe they too saw something like this long-snouted beast, thousands of years ago.

If you're convinced that people may have seen wolf-human hybrids in other realms, you may naturally wonder what shapes our consciousness could transform into when visiting these realms. After all, like the otherdimensional beings they see, shamans claim to take on an animal shape. When taking such a shape, perhaps we could travel among and affect the physical world, too, as wolves or other animal shapes.

CHAPTER ELEVEN

ASTRAL WEREWOLVES

Could shapeshifting be nothing more than a vivid out-of-body experience? Such a possibility was the basis for a novel that should be considered a classic of lycanthropy and shapeshifting: *Darker Than You Think*, by Jack Williamson. Published in 1948, this story almost takes for granted that shapeshifting is really astral in nature, and cleverly layers in some quantum mechanics for good measure and richer storytelling. The book is a good read and should serve as a change of pace for those who are tired of encountering the same themes in werewolf literature and movies.

Was Williamson ahead of his time? This chapter will explore the evidence behind how humans may have encountered those who are out of body, seeing them as living phantoms. Then we'll delve into the plentiful evidence that astral projection and astral shapeshifting may be more than just an interesting topic for a horror novel.

On now to the fourth and final type of werewolf we'll be examining in these pages.

SEEING DOUBLES

Lest you think this is an anticlimactic chapter where I say that lycanthropy is all an internal hallucination, I have to begin with something few people know even in the occult community. One of the first long-term, serious areas of study in so-called parapsychology didn't deal with a study of ghosts of the dead. It dealt with "phantasms" of the living.

Back in 1886, when the Society for Psychical Research was only a few years old, the topic of phantasms of the living was the subject of a two-volume study published by the SPR. Aptly titled *Phantasms of the Living*, the collection by Edmund Gurney, Frederick Meyers, and Frank Podmore put forth an overwhelming amount of evidence to back its main argument: the possibility that the living could see astral doubles of the living.

The primary type of event related in the study occurs when someone who is still living suffers some type of crisis. This event could range from a true near-death experience, in which the person loses consciousness, to a moment where a person merely thinks his or her life is in danger and retains consciousness—and everything in between. The astral or spiritual form of the person having the crisis then appears to a living friend or family member. Because of this typical feature in these cases, the phantasms of the living have been called *crisis apparitions* since the end of the nineteenth century.

The timing always works out in these tales. Exactly while the crisis is occurring, someone whom the sufferer cares about ends up seeing the sufferer's phantasm. Such a phantom can be either hyper-realistic to the point that the person viewing it actually believes the sufferer has stopped by for a visit, or can be so ghostly that the witness believes the sufferer must certainly be dead.

The person who suffered the trauma does not always have a memory of visiting this friend or relative. Usually, though, the sufferer recalls at least thinking about the person. For some reason, an unconscious desire to seek help from this person is enough to send something that can be perceived to the faraway friend or relative. Telepathy could be an explanation, with the person getting such a clear mental broadcast from the sufferer that they think they actually caught a glimpse. But the tangible-looking phantom stories seem to indicate that the sufferer sent something much more than just a thought. The sufferer could have sent his or her astral body.

Occult theories from almost every culture support the belief that humans have a subtle body or soul. This soul is believed by some cultures or mystical groups to travel outside the body every night during dreams. Most cultures and practitioners believe that astral travel occurs only under special mystical circumstances. Either way, if you believe in life after death or the unseen world, and that our minds are energy that cannot be created or destroyed, then that energy should be able to move about in a field of its own type. An astral body should be able to move freely about an astral plane or realm.

So far we've established that, according to eyewitnesses, people may be able to travel out of their bodies and appear to others during a crisis situation. On occasion, the form the phantoms appear in is actually one that resembles the crisis situation their living counterparts are experiencing. For example, someone might appear as a phantom with blood on her hands because the woman having the traumatic experience sees blood on her hands before passing out in a car accident. The blood is obviously not on the phantom or astral body (assuming that astral bodies exist, and that they are the explanation for phantoms of the living). The phantom blood is only there because our astral forms would have to be controllable in both movement and appearance by our minds. All signs point to this in the occult world. If you can think it, your astral body can resemble it, even if the form you're thinking of is of an animal instead of a human.

Trauma is not the only way to initiate an out-of-body experience. Many meditative and quasi-ritualistic techniques for inducing astral travel exist. All of these involve intense visualizations that lead to the sensation of awareness of a subtle or astral body, then to the feeling that this body is departing the physical one to begin its adventure. Put simply, imagining with clarity that astral traveling is happening leads to it happening.

Having a little intentional or accidental help with the imagining doesn't hurt, either . . .

FLYING OINTMENTS AND
DEVIL-FUELED TRANSFORMATIONS

Recall the ritual in chapter 5 for turning into a werewolf. In it, the practitioner is breathing in fumes from hallucinogenic herbs for a decent length of time. He or she is also working to a frenzy of exhaustion, and wearing a wolf skin. Imagine having all those elements working for you as you enter an altered state or out-of-body experience. Not only could you vividly imagine becoming a wolf, but the self-induced "crisis" of the ritual could also send your astral form off into the woods in wolf form to appear to someone.

Remarkably, Saint Augustine put forth the possibility of astral shapeshifting in his *City of God*. Even though the language is a little dense, I have decided to include the relevant theory here:

> *And indeed the demons, if they really do such things as these on which this discussion turns, do not create real substances, but only change the appearance of things created by the true God so as to make them seem to be what they are not. I cannot therefore believe that even the body, much less the mind, can really be changed into bestial forms and lineaments by any reason, art, or power of the demons; but the phantasm of a man, which even in thought or dreams goes through innumerable changes, may, when the man's senses are laid asleep or overpowered, be presented to the senses of others in a corporeal form, in some indescribable way unknown to me, so that men's bodies them-selves may lie somewhere, alive, indeed, yet with their senses locked up much more heavily and firmly than by sleep, while that phantasm, as it were embodied in the shape of some animal, may appear to the senses of others, and may even seem to the man himself to be changed, just as he may seem to himself in sleep to be so changed, and to bear burdens; and these burdens, if they are real substances, are borne by the demons, that men may be deceived by beholding at the same time the real substance of the burdens and the simulated bodies of the beasts of burden.*[1]

He doesn't claim to understand the process by which a form may astrally travel, but he points out how the whole thing could happen while the physical body lies in something heavier than sleep. He even remarkably relates a paranormal anecdote of such an astral transfor-mation:

> *For a certain man called Praestantius used to tell that it had happened to his father in his own house, that he took that poison in a piece of*

cheese, and lay in his bed as if sleeping, yet could by no means be aroused. But he said that after a few days he as it were woke up and related the things he had suffered as if they had been dreams, namely, that he had been made a sumpter horse, and, along with other beasts of burden, had carried provisions for the soldiers of what is called the Rhoetian Legion, because it was sent to Rhoetia. And all this was found to have taken place just as he told, yet it had seemed to him to be his own dream. And another man declared that in his own house at night, before he slept, he saw a certain philosopher, whom he knew very well, come to him and explain to him some things in the Platonic philosophy which he had previously declined to explain when asked. And when he had asked this philosopher why he did in his house what he had refused to do at home, he said, "I did not do it, but I dreamed I had done it." And thus what the one saw when sleeping was shown to the other when awake by a phantasmal image.[2]

The flying ointments allegedly used by witches to travel to visit the devil contained many of the same ingredients you read about in the werewolf ritual. The effects of these herbs, when they are taken in combination, range from hallucinations, to something called "twilight sleep," to various levels of poisoning. With just the right accompanying mixture, henbane and belladonna would have given an overall feeling of detachment and of flying. These are the exact sensations needed for a controlled out-of-body experience. Add the intention to travel as a witch or transform into a wolf, and you can make an argument that the person using the herbal mixture will either hallucinate that the travel has occurred, or will actually send his or her consciousness elsewhere.

It's hard to prove that someone's fantasies of flight or of running as a wolf have any external reality. Crisis apparitions that are observed seem to be a good start, as are experiments in which people who leave their body are asked to identify targets in another room. The problem with either of these will always be where the information is coming from. Is the witness seeing someone because they received a telepathic blast? Is the person allegedly traveling to another room really just reading the mind of the researcher? Pretty fantastic alternative explanations, sure, but proving the reality of telepathy would not prove that actual consciousness can travel in a possibly transformable shape.

Before we examine some claims—ancient and modern—of what astral werewolves can accomplish, let's cover just a little more astral theory so it all makes sense.

ASTRAL 101 AND SENDING OUT A LITTLE WOLF

When dealing with theories of the astral plane, you have to keep in mind that it's supposed to be a realm of creation. The prevailing idea is that not only can we move about in astral forms of our choosing (from glowing humanoid to wolf), but we can create external forms of astral "matter" as well. Most forms of magic that rely on visualization are said to take advantage of this principle. You imagine something clearly while building your psychodrama in a ritual. At the peak moment, you let go—and the imagined form is supposed to take on reality in the unseen astral world, fueled by the parts of your consciousness that the ritual allows you to tap. In time, the astral form you created is then supposed to manifest in the physical world, obeying physical laws to do so.

If you haven't tangoed with magic, the preceding explanation may sound bizarre. But even quantum mechanics allows for dominos of probability to fall and affect alternative realities in multidimensional theory. For example, you choose one street on your morning commute, and avoid the alternate universe where you're involved in a ten-car pileup on the other route. An astral form is said to take advantage of probabilities and paths of decision like this, eventually getting to a physical outcome that lets it come into being. If someone did a spell to keep you safe that morning, the spell could be the reason you chose the alternate route, for instance.

Astral forms created to accomplish a goal are sometimes called *thoughtforms*. These thoughtforms are typically not sensed by others until they manifest on the physical plane, because they are created as a means to an end. In a protection spell, you visualize a person as already being safe; you don't visualize the process of him or her becoming safer. That would limit the dominos the universe can tip over to set the right chain of events in motion. A properly created thoughtform only manifests physically.

What about viewing and interacting with other astral forms while they are still astral? As we saw with crisis apparitions, someone having an out-of-body experience—someone inhabiting the astral body that's already inside him or her—can occasionally be viewed by, or interact with, the living. This implies that someone traveling in wolf form may be perceived by wide-awake individuals, possibly accounting for werewolf sightings around the world.

Another type of astral form is one that is created and takes on a life of its own. In Tibet there is the practice of creating a *tulpa*, a sort of manufactured spirit that can independently act and be seen. Alexandra David-Néel, a Belgian explorer, spent time in Tibet and witnessed the creation of a tulpa that looked like a monk—which was clearly visible to many individuals. Most uncanny about David-Néel's account of the experience is that she was never told this was a unique occurrence. Creating visible tulpas is a part of life to these Tibetan monks, and is only one of the impressive feats they master as part of their training.

Creating a visible tulpa is said to take a lot of effort and a strong intent. According to a well-known occult author from the first half of the twentieth century, Dion Fortune, it is possible to accidentally create something like a tulpa or an astral form that others can see. As with a crisis apparition, such a manufactured being can be the result of strong emotions, even though the intent was not to have it be visible to others. In Dion Fortune's case, the being she manufactured was, you guessed it, a wolf.

Dion Fortune's Astral Wolf

Just being a well-known occultist involved in a secret society doesn't make one perfect. No snarky comments, please, I'm talking about Dion Fortune here. Despite being the founding member of what would become the Society of the Inner Light, Fortune admitted to having moments of less-than-light thoughts. One such tale is related in her excellent book *Psychic Self-Defence*.

In the tale, Fortune admits to creating a thoughtform, or "elemental," when in a less-than-pure state of mind. She even calls it a werewolf experience, so it's just too perfect an example to leave out. Fortune had been lying in bed, brooding about someone who hurt her. She was considering retaliating against this person, and her thoughts started drifting to how, long ago, people who were in a rage really knew how to let loose. She started thinking of berserkers, and of the Norse wolf god Fenris. Drifting halfway to sleep put Fortune into an altered state of consciousness:

> *Immediately I felt a curious drawing-out sensation from my solar plexus, and there materialised beside me on the bed a large wolf. It was a well-materialised ectoplasmic form . . . I could distinctly feel its back pressing against me as it lay beside me on the bed as a large dog might.*
>
> *I knew nothing about the art of making elementals at that time, but had accidentally stumbled upon the right method—the brooding highly charged with emotion, the invocation of the appropriate natural force, and the condition between sleeping and waking . . .* [3]

Having been in the occult scene for some time, Fortune knew that she had to take control of this wolf she created in anger. The ancient legend of the clay man that a rabbi creates and loses control over, called the Golem, is a warning to mystics about what happens if creatures are allowed to roam free. They become like Frankenstein's monster in horror movies, roaming out of control.

Fortune decided to try and command the beast, which must have been getting stronger by the moment. It turned its snout to her and began to snarl. She could even see its teeth. Fortune decided to get the upper hand and elbowed it in the "ectoplasmic ribs," saying, "If you can't behave yourself, you will have to go on the floor."

The wolf did end up on the floor, then took off through the wall at the northern corner of the room, perhaps to tie into Fortune's thought of Fenris's region of origin. In keeping with the point of this chapter, this wolf that Fortune created was seen by others, too. The next morning someone who lived in the house told Fortune that she dreamed of wolves and woke up in the middle of the night to "see the eyes of a wild animal shining in the darkness in the corner of her room."

The story doesn't end like a horror movie, as the wolf never goes out and ravages the person who wronged Fortune. Instead, she ends up calling forth the thing to draw its astral essence into herself and dissolve it. When it returns the next night, again from the northern corner, the wolf is so realistic that Fortune can even smell it in the room! Fortune manages to do what she intended, pulling it in without becoming more wolflike herself (although that would have been a really great story to include!).

Fortune's story—complete with its wolf creature that she can see, hear, smell, and feel—is a good example of just how real an astral form can seem to an eyewitness.

WEREWOLF WARRIORS

In Italy, there was a unique group of good witches from the sixteenth and seventeenth centuries. I say *unique* because the word was rarely used by the populace for beneficial magic practitioners back then. These "good walkers," or *Benandanti*, were people who claimed that they traveled out of body to battle *streghe*, or evil witches. Such astral battles were not unique to these warring factions of witches. As it turns out, around the same period of time, in 1691, a man from the Baltic province of Livonia believed that he also traveled out of body to do such battle against evil magic-wielders. The difference is this man, named Thiess, believed that he traveled in the astral form of a werewolf.

Oh, and to add a final bit of color to his testimony, Thiess claimed these battles took place in no less than Hell itself!

In his eighties at the time of his trial, Thiess was surprisingly old to be a werewolf of folklore. He claimed that his transformation was necessary to battle the evil sorcerer Skeistan Rein and his companions, who had stolen wheat, various livestock, and other essentials from the village. It is unclear how astral forms of sorcerers were able to carry such physical food and living things with them. The court records do not add any theory from the time to the testimony. Perhaps Thiess believed that the sorcerers were taking some kind of astral essence essential for the town's ability to continue growing healthy crops and maintaining livestock.

Astral theories in the occult world are not exactly in short supply. One of the most prevalent theories is that whatever happens on the astral plane will ultimately manifest on the physical plane. This could explain why stealing astral forms of crops could be construed as an evil form of sorcery designed to bring famine to an area. This would be analogous, in a ritual, to imagining a person getting sick in hopes that a real illness will come to pass.

The astral theory of manifestation also seems to apply to another interesting piece of testimony in the case. Thiess claimed that in the underworld battleground, Skeistan smashed Thiess in his wolf-form face with a bizarre weapon, which was composed of a broom handle covered with horses' tails. When he returned to his human and physical form, Thiess had a matching wound on his nose.

Note that this kind of astral-into-physical wound is the most common complaint of people who claim that something phantomlike is attacking them in their bed at night. In such cases, the idea is that the phantom malicious entity is really hitting the victim on his or her astral body. Whether they try to get back to sleep or get up immediately afterward, these victims will find welts or scratches on their body that match where the being made contact with them.

Thiess claimed that he was made into a werewolf by a man he called a "scoundrel of Magdeburg." The transformation spell this scoundrel used was as simple as any encountered in folklore. The scoundrel effected the transformation by blowing on Thiess's drink three times, and then saying the following words:

May what happened to me happen to you.

The belief was that once this charm was completed, Thiess would become a werewolf, and the other man, who was also a werewolf, would be free of his condition.

Despite Thiess claiming many times that he had to become part of the unseen world to find the secret door to Hell, his method of transformation matches with one of the alleged physical ones we've looked at. He claimed to strip off his clothes and hide them in the bushes, and then put on a wolf skin to initiate the transformation. I'd say this strongly supports the theory that wearing a wolf skin adds to the psychodrama needed to astrally transform into a wolf.

Thiess claimed that these battles happened about three times a year, usually on the Feasts of Saint Lucy and Saint John, and on the Pentecost. These seemed to be the nights that the sorcerers took the village's essentials of livelihood to the underworld. Note that the Feast of Saint Lucy is December 13, and Thiess actually refers to it as a night leading up to Christmas, once again bringing some lycanthropic significance to the holiday.

Aside from the mark people claimed to see on Thiess's nose after the sorcerer hit him astrally (and this can be explained by someone having really hit him), there is no physical evidence that the old fellow was able to accomplish the feats he claimed. The trial seems centered on Thiess's heresy more than any real actions that brought about public attention. One bit of testimony sums up his views on why lycanthropy is anything but heresy. As translated by Claude Lecouteux in *Witches, Werewolves, and Fairies*, the judges ask Thiess a straightforward question and get an equally direct response:

Q: *How can your soul go to God given that you do not serve Him but the devil, that you do not go to church, at least to confession, and that you do not take communion, as you yourself admit?*

R: *Werewolves do not serve the devil because they rob him of what the sorcerers bring him; that is why the devil hates them, cannot stand them, and has them hunted like dogs, with great cracks of his iron whips . . . Everything werewolves do is for the good of men . . .* [4]

As Thiess hadn't really done anything but say some blasphemous things in a courtroom, the court was merciful and sentenced him to ten lashes.

This legend could be yet another form of mania, and the underworld wars he describes did seem not to have had much tangible effect on the physical plane. No one actually lost any physical wheat or cattle, and Thiess didn't return any such stolen goods physically.

The best evidence to support the astral-transformation theory would have to be a little more modern, and would need to suggest that not only could the astral form be seen, but also be seen to interact with the environment.

For example, what if someone left their body in astral-wolf form and then killed an animal? Read on . . .

SOLSTICE-NIGHT RITES IN SWEDEN

The following experience is from a good friend of mine best known for his company Sabretooth, which makes fangs for the mortal blood-drinker community. It's no surprise that Father Sebastiaan seeks out bizarre experiences, but this one kind of found him:

This is the first time I have shared this publicly.

In the spring of 2004, I was at a music festival and met a Swedish girl who was very lovely, with fangs, blonde streaks in her hair, and, of course, a cowboy hat. This gal (M for the story) had a strong fascination with tattoos, and werewolves were their primary subject matter. Soon after the festival and a night of partying, my friends put me in M's car and I woke up on the ferry going to Scandinavia for the first time.

We spent two lovely weeks together in Gothenburg, and during this time I was privileged to meet many unique individuals, including one at a local occult bookshop. I'll call him Cass here. He knew me from my writings and my work as a fangsmith.

After my return to Amsterdam, Cass and I began corresponding. Cass told me of the mushrooms that the old Viking Berserkers employed, and that shapeshifting was something entirely spiritual which could affect the physical world. He then invited me to come back to

Sweden to witness a special summer-solstice ritual involving nothing less than "true lycanthropy," Scandinavian style.

Cass explained that they would use a mushroom to mentally adjust to the first steps of transformation, and that everyone has the ability to shapeshift. The mushroom is called Fly Agaric, or Amanita muscaria. Being a resident of Amsterdam at the time, I already had legal access to (and experience with) natural psychedelics. My curiosity was piqued.

I boarded a flight for Norway, and upon arrival met my ride to Sweden: three fairly large blond men and Cass. They were excited to know I had brought my fang kit to begin their transformations with a little cosmetic help. They believe the psychological aspect of coming closer to a wolf in your outer appearance assists in the ritual of transformation.

We drove toward the Swedish border and beyond, far north. I asked if these guys were members of Dragon Rouge, a local esoteric order with which I feel a strong resonance. One said that he once was a member, but that this current group was more private. After about a dozen hours in transit, and a briefing on their lycanthropic philosophy, we were deep in the forest where the sun would never set at this time of year. Cass brought me to a campsite to meet a half-dozen other people, for a total of eleven.

The largest of my three drivers, who called himself Thorn, mentioned to me that we would start the ritual around midnight, and that we couldn't eat much beforehand. I had my portable fang kit on me and I was able to get about five pairs finished in the time we had.

Around 11 p.m. we began with a drum circle and meditations, accompanied by only a light meal of mead and beef. We drank and then we were handed our mushrooms in little cakes. One of the two ladies in the group started playing a flute, and we began dancing. The "priest," whose name I cannot remember, wore large bear skins, chainmail, and *a sword. I was instructed to remove my clothes as I danced, and to welcome in my spirit animal.*

What happened next I can only remember as if it were a dream. My point of view during this other state was that of a great cat, running through the forest. I felt compelled to do so, almost like a marionette. I was not alone in this run. I recall glimpses of a pack of wolves and bears running with me. We were on a hunt. I even recall using the beast's vocal cords. When I woke up from that run, I was covered with dirt and blood. I looked around and saw that some of the other members were still on the ground, howling or rolling in primal positions.

Thorn came to me and put out his long arm. He was covered with blood and dirt as well, with an almost wolf-like appearance in his face and spirit. He smiled, and I could see he'd broken off his fangs.

Evidently we had only been in the "transformation" for about two hours, and it was almost 2:30 a.m. The sun was clearly shining, and we had gained our most primal experiences during what little darkness we had.

Cass asked me if I remembered anything, and I told him about my run as a cat. He said we went on a spiritual hunt. Before me was a deer, which he claimed was in our path on this hunt. We began to feast and drink mead.

The conversations that took place over the next 48 hours of my stay in Sweden I dare not repeat. Beyond these memories, I do have one souvenir: an intriguing scar on my ribcage that I can't explain.

Not a bad way to spend a solstice, right? Seriously, assuming that none of the ritual participants physically went hunting either while on the mushroom, or because they secretly didn't take the mushroom to perpetrate a fraud, this is a significant experience. If the participants in this ritual were actually able to hunt and kill an animal while they were in astral form, then even the most fantastic of werewolf sightings would have a possible explanation.

Without any controls in place, we'll never know if the kill did occur astrally, but obtaining such proof would be awe-inspiring. Guess I have to attend the next solstice rite they have . . .

Note that the practitioners of this solstice rite may have chosen a particularly dramatic way to go about it, considering the location and the date, but they are not exactly unique in modern times.

OTHERKIN THERIANS

Earlier in the book we talked about how *therianthropes* ("beast people") used to be a general term to describe werecreatures that were not necessarily werewolves. In recent years, the term has been adopted by subgroups of otherkin to describe their particular spiritual practice. Otherkin in general closely identify with a mythical creature of some sort, and believe that they are the real-world manifestation of such a creature, minus the fictional hype. This could include everything from fairies without wings, to vampires without fangs (at least not ones they were born with), to—I swear I'm not making this up—dragons without, well, anything dragonlike at all.

The type of otherkin of interest here is the *therian*. These folks don't usually believe they can transform physically into other creatures, but they do believe they have a solid connection to a particular animal and its nature. Some of them only take this as far as living close to nature and enjoying what they feel are heightened awareness of their surroundings, better senses, and the ability to interact with actual creatures around them. Some therians go a bit further.

This chapter is about the possibility of perceived werewolf transformation and sightings being explained by astral projection in wolf form. Some therians strive to achieve just such experiences on a regular basis, and they argue that therians have always been around and always misunderstood. It certainly is possible that folks like Thiess were therians who took it a bit too far; and skinwalkers, too, may be perfectly legit examples of therians from before the time the cultural and spiritual movement became aware that it was a cultural and spiritual movement.

Occasionally I hear from a reader who may be in league with the therian lifestyle but perhaps hasn't heard the term. Here is a perfect example, and one that helps along our exploration of astral shapeshifting:

> I have spent over 10 years trying to learn how to shapeshift correctly. On several different occasions I have had "strange dreams" (that's what I call them) where I'm someplace doing something, but as a cat. Not only that but I have actually been accused by several different people of shapeshifting into a cat, and scaring them during the night while they are in their homes.
>
> In my dreams I see, hear, smell, and taste everything as if I was there, but of course my body is in bed. Friends, and enemies, have called the day following saying things such as, "I know you sent an evil cat after me" or "A strange cat cornered me in my house last night," when they do not own cats. Ironically, I know everything as soon as I wake up, so their call just proves to me that I'm not completely crazy. However, I just let others think that they are nuts, or that it was the doings of witchery.
>
> The only other person I have ever told about this is my fiancée. So we always get a kick out of it when it happens. Unfortunately, I haven't mastered control of this gift.

This book isn't really a how-to on adopting an alternative lifestyle. But if you feel the need to dig up information on how to join the pack, so to speak, it's out there (those in the movement seem to favor books by Lupa, especially *A Field Guide to Otherkin* and *Fang and Fur, Blood and Bone*). I'm all about the power of psychodrama, and if someone feels that the only way to connect with the unseen is in animal form, then he or she should feel free to seek out others who practice such a lifestyle and see what's involved.

Again, I don't claim to be part of a therian movement and can't advise anyone on what it's like to live such a lifestyle. However, if you want to explore the possibility of giving astral transformation at least a quick try, you might find the following tale of particular interest.

THE WEREWOLF OF WASHINGTON SQUARE

Not all astral-werewolf experiences are part of rituals with obvious wolf elements or wolf-transformation intentions. In the 1920s, an interesting occult experiment went awry not too far away from me, in New York City's Washington Square. The person heading the experiment was William Seabrook, an occult explorer who was admirably honest about both his successes and failures with all manner of activities, even to the point of occasionally discounting what may have been valid evidence. Despite his sometimes throwing the baby out with the bathwater, Seabrook's 1940 book *Witchcraft: Its Power in the World Today* is a must-read if you can find a copy (paperback copies from the sixties and later turn up in used bookstores from time to time). Look past the fact that it was titled back in the day when the *W* word meant something a bit different from what it means now. This book was published before the creation and popularization of the "Old Religion," and is really a collection of fascinating experiences involving everything from voodoo to necromancy to astral projection. It's this last one that is a component in the werewolf experience he provides in the book.

One night Seabrook proposed an experiment with a visiting Russian aristocrat named Nastatia Filipovna. She was a refugee of sorts who had dropped her title and tried to blend in to American society. Filipovna claimed to have known the Mad Monk Rasputin, one of the most colorful and bizarre characters of mystical history. Seabrook found Filipovna to be a little on the savage side, which is an interesting trait to find in a member of the upper class. Seabrook theorized that this rough nature might have contributed somewhat to how she reacted to the events that came next.

The experiment they tried that night in 1923 had to do with meditating on characters of the *I Ching*, or "Yi King," as Seabrook spelled it. The *I Ching* is an ancient Chinese text that contains a series of symbols that are supposed to help reveal the order behind seemingly random events. When used in divination, the *I Ching* symbols or hexagrams are cast using some type of object or objects, usually coins or yarrow stalks, and the resulting symbols are interpreted. In Seabrook's account, they had obtained an odd medium: dark-colored tortoise-shell wands, along with instructions on how to cast them to end up with the symbols or hexagrams.

Typically, once you cast and get a hexagram, you can interpret it using the *I Ching*'s detailed descriptions, much as people do with a book when first learning what each card of the tarot means. Seabrook's experiment did not use the ancient symbols for divination, though. Rather, he set up a form of pathworking to get Filipovna to astrally project through the cast symbol in hopes of seeing what types of relevant or irrelevant experiences she would have.

Seabrook took Filipovna to his friend Bannister's apartment. Bannister had the place decorated in suitable occult regalia, including statues from various ancient cultures, and incense filling the room with consciousness-altering scents and carbon monoxide. Not a bad psychodramatic setting, but still, there were no wolf references present among all the occult trappings in the room.

It should be noted that Seabrook did not preselect for use that night a particular hexagram or symbol from the *I Ching*. As part of the experiment he randomly cast the little tortoise-shell wands he had bought in the city earlier, thereby forming the hexagram called *ko*. Seabrook then had Filipovna relax and meditate on the shape, which is shown on the following page.

She was then told to close her eyes and imagine the shape before her, letting the hexagram grow in size to become a large door. The final step was one that Seabrook doubted would have any effect. Filipovna was to let her astral body travel through the glyph. Seabrook didn't believe that popping out in an impromptu manner like this was possible.

Nothing happened for over an hour, and Filipovna started to complain about being uncomfortable. She said her body was going numb from sitting on the floor for so long. Gradually she settled down on her "haunches," with her head sagging. An interesting physical position to assume, and one that could have helped foster what came next.

Well after an hour had passed, Filipovna said that the door was starting to open. Peering through with her astral senses (her eyes were still closed), Filipovna saw that the portal led outdoors into a snowy field. She said she was going through the door. The moon was out in her vision, and she described lying down in what didn't seem to imply a human form:

> I am lying naked in a fur coat . . . and I am warm in the snow . . . flat with my belly and chin on the snow I lie.[5]

She soon after started sounding puzzled, describing more details of what her astral senses were experiencing in the winter realm:

I'm running, on my hands and feet, lightly . . . I'm running lightly like the wind . . . how good the snow smells! And there's another good smell. Ah ah! Faster . . . faster . . . [6]

Filipovna then started panting heavily and yelping like a wolf. Bannister was quite shocked by the way she started writhing, telling Seabrook he thought Filipovna was actually transforming into a wolf. Seabrook told him that it wasn't physically happening, but did see how such an experience would have landed them all in an Inquisition bonfire had someone observed them centuries ago.

When Filipovna came out of the experience, she made an almost comical request of the two men staring at her in amazement. She claimed to be hungry. Weeks later, she wanted to try the experience again. Seabrook was no doubt thoroughly satisfied of her savage nature by this point.

You'll note that I didn't share what the *ko* hexagram means yet. Remember, Seabrook cast it at random and didn't tell Filipovna what the result was, probably to maintain some skeptical ground to judge what she claimed to see. It turns out that the meaning of the *ko* hexagram could have some significance to what ended up happening. Primarily, the symbol refers to an animal's pelt, and to molting or undergoing some kind of change. The Legge translation of the *I Ching* adds some ominous snippets to describe *ko* as well:

The great man (producing his changes) as the tiger (does when he) changes (his stripes) . . . the superior man producing his changes as the leopard (does when he) changes (his spots), while small men change their faces (and show their obedience). To go forward (now) would lead to evil . . . [7]

That Filipovna wasn't told any of this beforehand is certainly intriguing.

Perhaps you're considering a meditation on *ko*, and would like to try imagining that you too are moving through a giant version of it floating in the distance.

Please don't!

Okay, I'm kidding. This type of pathworking is actually a good way to learn the art of astral travel, and has been practiced with other symbols in the past, including Eastern tattwas, Asian ideograms of import, and tarot. You can try this experiment on its own, as Seabrook did, or you can combine it with everything from a wolf skin to the entire werewolf ritual given in chapter 5.

Just be sure to account for neighborhood livestock before you go astrally jumping through the hexagram, and be sure to write me if you manage to transform back.

By trying an astral transformation, after all, you may be joining the ranks of the only type of supernatural shapeshifters ever to exist.

CONCLUSION

Kiowa's heart is no longer beating. At least, he does not believe it is. His breathing has stopped as well. He must be dead, watching this all happen behind eyes that no one has closed yet.

The creature's snout has fully lowered through the hole now, revealing one red eye. Kiowa is certain it is putting off its own light, and it is not the fire below reflecting. With a slow turn of its head, the creature brings the other bloody orb around to fix Kiowa with a stare that no natural wolf could ever match.

It is human. It is . . . familiar?

Two heartbeats pass. Kiowa is certain once again that he is alive. For now.

The beast opens its mouth and slowly exhales. A gray powder sprinkles down out of its muzzle. The powder reflects the firelight as each grain tumbles in slow motion toward the flames. When the first bit of the powder makes contact with the fire, green sparks appear.

Kiowa smells something foul filling the room. But he cannot move away from the horrible aroma of decaying bodies. The eyes hold him still.

The head moves lower and the cloud of powder ceases its flow out of the beast's muzzle. Both of the wolf's ears appear, instantly. Kiowa thinks it odd that they do not bend as they pass through the hole. A funny detail to notice, moments before death.

As he continues to stare into the wolf's eyes, Kiowa thinks of Uncle. It has grown silent outside. He won't even hear the chanting one last time before this monster finishes descending and eats him.

The thing begins to breathe loudly, as if answering Kiowa's wish for Uncle's chanting with a its own, more terrible noise.

Uncle stays in his mind. Uncle's teachings. Uncle's . . . gift?

Kiowa forces himself to look away from the red eyes and reaches down his shirt. Hanging there is a small medicine bag containing a very special ingredient Uncle had prepared for his little "sleeping wolf."

With a speed Kiowa didn't know he had, he tears the medicine bag from the cord around his neck and holds it out toward the beast.

Kiowa's hand feels as if it is burning from the inside—as if an energy within him is activating the special ingredient inside the medicine bag.

"Wolf gall!" Kiowa yells.

The wolf's breathing silences. Its eyes fade from a fiery red to a light brown. Kiowa knows those eyes.

The wolf vanishes.

From behind him, Uncle's voice: "You are ready, sleeping wolf."

Kiowa turns to see the familiar brown eyes, and knows who the next shaman in the family is to be.

If there's one thing I hope you take away from this book, it's that in the world of the hidden or the occult, alternative explanations are all we have. By their nature, these mysteries demand we try to illuminate what they mean to us, or they wouldn't be mysteries.

I've tried to remain fair and objective here, as I always strive to do in both books and life. In doing so, I hope I didn't come across as too harsh a critic of any believer's worldview, or too insane a researcher for those whose worldview holds no acceptance of such strange things. This is an honest search for hidden truths, and I don't feel a need to give any apologies.

Seven occult books into this career, and I remain a skeptic in the true sense of the word. Rather than repeat myself on what this word means, I'll word it another way. A skeptic is a person with an open mind who challenges everything, and happily accepts the ideas that begin to filter above the murky waters of those concepts that don't hold up to the challenges. Those who publish works as skeptics rarely hold to these ideals, instead establishing unrealistic, flawed criteria of proof. The pseudo-skeptics then happily fail at meeting their own criteria, "proving" their points.

When it comes to ghosts, we can't be waiting for the day that a dead guy floats into a lab and asks to be studied. With werewolves, it can't be the day we shoot a lycanthrope with a silver bullet and haul her carcass onto a talk show (although she may have changed into a dead gal by this point).

Are werewolves real? I promised that the evidence might surprise you, and perhaps it has. My final conclusion is that most of the evidence I've found and shared seems to support the idea that our consciousness can take on forms and move about the world. Further, the experiences suggest that there may be conscious beings on other planes of reality doing the same kind of moving about. As conscious beings ourselves, we're equipped to sometimes perceive those traveling forms for the transformed beings they are (or, in the case of otherdimensional beings, for the inherently alien ones that they are). Remember the dichotomy from this book's introduction:

Finding that a belief in something is shared around the world seems to imply it is true . . . yet finding contradictions in said belief's details makes it hard to accept the mystery at hand.

We have to consider why people all around the world have experienced something like shapeshifting werewolves, or creatures that seem to always be in an animal-human hybrid form. People all around the world share the same type of consciousness.

Science is not exactly bearing out the astral theory of werewolves just yet (or any theory of werewolves, for that matter). I can live with the fact that astral travel is still not appearing in quantum-mechanics journals directly. That's not to say science isn't proving indirectly a few key ingredients required for astral travel to be a possibility. We know that in at least some experimental setups, our concepts of information and how it travels around the universe are not quite what we once thought. Look up *entanglement* in a physics book if you don't believe me, or wait until my next book. Also, the concept of other dimensions is becoming the favorite explanation for many quantum theories. Why not the possibility of information or other intelligent beings moving about in those other dimensions?

But don't take my word for any of this. I could be wrong about my nonphysical explanation for werewolves, even though they remain quite intangible as far as capture goes. Next time you see something furry in the light of a full moon, you may want to reconsider before you reach out and poke it.

NOTES

CHAPTER ONE: SEPARATING FACT FROM FICTION

1. The closest candidate for the ultimate piece of werewolf literature was a 1933 novel by Guy Endore called *The Were-wolf of Paris*. Werewolf cinema and even future horror novels would have evolved in a far different way had screenwriters taken a little more from Endore's book. Endore got some folklore right, down to the obscure belief that being born on Christmas predisposed one to becoming a werewolf. Further, he captured the sense

of madness that surrounds some of the more famous werewolf cases. Lasting fame eluded the book, however, despite it being the loose basis for the 1961 film *The Curse of the Werewolf.* Your chances of finding someone today who has heard of this noteworthy work are slim; your chances of finding someone who has actually read it seem as slim as being bitten by a werewolf!

2. Fred H. Harrington and Paul C. Paquet, eds., *Wolves of the World: Perspectives of Behavior, Ecology, and Conservation* (Park Ridge, NJ: Noyes Publications, 1982), 318–19.

3. The first movie to spread the idea of a bite turning a victim into a werewolf was 1935's *Werewolf of London,* which makes one wonder if the writers had vampires in mind when writing their screenplay. The visuals in that film were reminiscent of vampires, with Dr. Wilfred Glendon looking more like a vampire with poor grooming habits than a wolf. Of course in the more famous classic, *The Wolf Man,* the theory of one werewolf creating another by bite has a comical flaw: the werewolf that bit Larry Talbot looked like a large wolf . . . yet ended up turning Talbot into an anthropomorphic werewolf—the classic wolf man. Watch the scene in slow motion, and you can see it's clearly a wolf puppet of some sort—not Bela Lugosi in makeup.

CHAPTER TWO: WEREWOLF BELIEFS FROM AROUND THE WORLD

1. Stephanie Dalley, *Myths from Mesopotamia* (Oxford: Oxford University Press, 2000), 53.

2. Ibid., 79.

3. Charles Francis Horne, ed., *The Sacred Books and Early Literature of the East* (New York: Parke, Austin, and Lipscomb, 1917), 230.

4. George M. Lamsa, trans., *Holy Bible: From the Ancient Eastern Text* (San Francisco: Harper & Row, 1985), 889.

5. Saint Augustine, *The City of God, Volume 2* (Edinburgh, Scotland: T & T Clark, 1888), 236.

CHAPTER THREE: INVOLUNTARY WEREWOLVES OF LEGEND

1. Dylan Evans, *Placebo: Mind Over Matter in Modern Medicine* (New York: Oxford University Press, 2004), 1.

CHAPTER FOUR: VOLUNTARY WEREWOLVES OF LEGEND

1. Gabriel Ronay, *The Dracula Myth* (London: W. H. Allen, 1972), 15.

2. Montague Summers, *The Werewolf* (New Hyde Park, NY: University Books, 1966), 253.

CHAPTER FIVE: WEREWOLF RITUALS

1. Elliott O'Donnell, *Werwolves* (London: Methuen and Co., 1912), 55.

2. Ibid., 55–59.

3. Ibid., 240.

4. Ibid., 275.

5. Sabine Baring-Gould, *The Book of Werewolves* (New York: Causeway Books, 1973), 117.

6. Montague Summers (1966), 98.

7. Hedwig Schleiffer, ed., *Narcotic Plants of the Old World Used in Rituals and Everyday Life* (Monticello, NY: Lubrecht & Cramer, 1979), 139.

CHAPTER SIX: KILLING AND CURING WEREWOLVES

1. Sabine Baring-Gould (1973), 55.

2. Elliott O'Donnell (1912), 89.

3. Ibid., 90.

4. Ibid., 221.

5. Ibid., 222.

CHAPTER NINE: NATIVE AMERICAN BELIEFS AND SHAMANISM

1. Alberta Hannum, *Spin a Silver Dollar* (New York: Viking, 1945), 82.

CHAPTER TEN: OTHERDIMENSIONAL BEINGS

1. Rick Strassman, *DMT: The Spirit Molecule* (Rochester, VT: Park Street Press, 2001), 341–42.

CHAPTER ELEVEN: ASTRAL WEREWOLVES

1. Saint Augustine (1888), 236–37.

2. Ibid., 237.

3. Dion Fortune, *Psychic Self-Defense* (San Francisco: Red Wheel/ Weiser, 2001), 39.

4. Claude Lecouteux, *Witches, Werewolves and Fairies* (Rochester, VT: Inner Traditions, 2003), 173.

5. William Seabrook, *Witchcraft: Its Power in the World Today* (New York: Lancer Books, 1968), 153–54.

6. Ibid., 154.

7. James Legge, trans., *The Sacred Books of China* (New York: Charles Scribner's Sons, 1899), 168.

BIBLIOGRAPHY

Augustine, Saint. *The City of God, Volume 2.* Edinburgh, Scotland: T & T Clark, 1888.

Baring-Gould, Sabine. *The Book of Werewolves.* New York: Causeway Books, 1973.

Burgard, Matthias. *Das Monster von Morbach.* Münster, Germany: Waxmann, 2008.

Dalley, Stephanie. *Myths from Mesopotamia.* Oxford: Oxford University Press, 2000.

Endore, Guy. *The Werewolf of Paris.* New York: Farrar & Rinehart, 1933.

Evans, Dylan. *Placebo: Mind Over Matter in Modern Medicine.* New York: Oxford University Press, 2004.

Fortune, Dion. *Psychic Self-Defense*. San Francisco: Red Wheel/Weiser, 2001.

Godfrey, Linda S. *The Beast of Bray Road: Tailing Wisconsin's Werewolf*. Black Earth, WI: Prairie Oak Press, 2003.

Haddock, Deborah Bray. *The Dissociative Identity Disorder Sourcebook*. Chicago: Contemporary Books, 2001.

Hancock, Graham. *Supernatural: Meetings with the Ancient Teachers of Mankind*. London: Century, 2005.

Hannum, Alberta. *Spin a Silver Dollar*. New York: Viking, 1945.

Harrington, Fred H., and Paul C. Paquet, eds. *Wolves of the World: Perspectives of Behavior, Ecology, and Conservation*. Park Ridge, NJ: Noyes Publications, 1982.

Horne, Charles Francis, ed. *The Sacred Books and Early Literature of the East*. New York: Parke, Austin, and Lipscomb, 1917.

Hufford, David J. *The Terror That Comes in the Night: An Experience-Centered Study of Supernatural Assault Traditions*. Philadelphia: University of Pennsylvania Press, 1982.

Lamsa, George M., trans. *Holy Bible: From the Ancient Eastern Text*. San Francisco: Harper & Row, 1985

Lecouteux, Claude. *Witches, Werewolves and Fairies*. Rochester, VT: Inner Traditions, 2003.

Legge, James, trans. *The Sacred Books of China*. New York: Charles Scribner's Sons, 1899.

Lupa. *A Field Guide to Otherkin*. Stafford, UK: Immanion Press, 2007.

———. *Fang and Fur, Blood and Bone*. Stafford, UK: Immanion Press, 2006.

Moselhy, Hamdy F. "Lycanthropy: New Evidence of Its Origin." *Psychopathology* 32, no. 4 (1999): 173–76.

O'Donnell, Elliott. *Werwolves*. London: Methuen and Co., 1912.

Otten, Charlotte F., ed. *A Lycanthropy Reader: Werewolves in Western Culture*. Syracuse, NY: Syracuse University Press, 1986.

Pinchbeck, Daniel. *Breaking Open the Head*. New York: Broadway Books, 2002.

Ronay, Gabriel. *The Dracula Myth*. London: W. H. Allen, 1972.

Seabrook, William. *Witchcraft: Its Power in the World Today*. New York: Lancer Books, 1968. First published in 1940.

Schleiffer, Hedwig, ed. *Narcotic Plants of the Old World Used in Rituals and Everyday Life*. Monticello, NY: Lubrecht & Cramer, 1979.

Sidky, H. *Witchcraft, Lycanthropy, Drugs, and Disease: An Anthropological Study of the European Witch-Hunts*. New York: Peter Lang, 1997.

Strassman, Rick. *DMT: The Spirit Molecule*. Rochester, VT: Park Street Press, 2001.

Summers, Montague. *The Werewolf*. New Hyde Park, NY: University Books, 1966. First published in 1933.

Thompson, R. Campbell. *The Devils and Evil Spirits of Babylonia*. London: Luzac, 1903–04 (published in two volumes).

Williamson, Jack. *Darker Than You Think*. New York: Orb, 1999. First published in 1948.

INDEX

Wolf Man, The (1941 film), 5, 69, 182

wolf skin, 26–27, 53–54, 63, 67–69, 71, 88–89, 128, 131, 133, 156, 164, 175

wound, telltale, 82–84, 90

Y

yee naaldlooshii, 131

Z

zoanthropy, 110

TO WRITE TO THE AUTHOR

If you wish to contact the author or would like more information about this book, please write to the author in care of Llewellyn Worldwide and we will forward your request. Both the author and publisher appreciate hearing from you and learning of your enjoyment of this book and how it has helped you. Llewellyn Worldwide cannot guarantee that every letter written to the author can be answered, but all will be forwarded. Please write to:

Konstantinos
℅ Llewellyn Worldwide Ltd.
2143 Wooddale Drive
Woodbury, MN 55125-2989

Please enclose a self-addressed stamped envelope for reply, or $1.00 to cover costs. If outside the USA, enclose an international postal reply coupon.

Many of Llewellyn's authors have websites with additional information and resources. For more information, please visit our website at http://www.llewellyn.com.

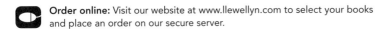

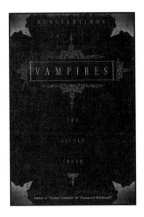

Vampires
The Occult Truth
KONSTANTINOS

Tales of black-caped blood suckers and life-stealing phantoms have fascinated us for centuries. *Vampires: The Occult Truth* uncovers the chilling truth about the legend that refuses to die.

Here is convincing evidence that vampires really exist. The actual facts are stranger than anything you may have read, heard, or imagined! Konstantinos presents firsthand accounts of encounters with vampires and vampirism of all types—the ancient undead of folklore, contemporary mortal blood drinkers, and the most dangerous of all: psychic vampires who intentionally drain the life force from their victims.

978-1-56718-380-1, 208 pp., 6 x 9   **$14.95**

To order, call 1-877-NEW-WRLD
Prices subject to change without notice
Order at Llewellyn.com 24 hours a day, 7 days a week!

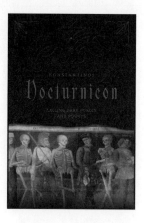

Nocturnicon
Calling Dark Forces and Powers

KONSTANTINOS

Take a thrilling walk on the dark side with Konstantinos! The author of *Werewolves: The Occult Truth* and several other books presents a collection of magickal techniques for working with dark forces. Developed and tested by Konstantinos, these rites and rituals have proven to be quite powerful in harnessing nocturnal energies—even helping the author overcome a serious medical condition in a miraculous recovery that shocked doctors.

Drawn from diverse sources—ceremonial magick, folk magick, ancient Greek ritual, and divination—the techniques in *Nocturnicon* enable magicians and novices to conjure and control primal energies, thoughtforms, Lovecraftian entities, egregores, sigils, and other forces. Those attracted to the dark mysteries will relish Konstantinos' bold exploration of sex magick, death magick, altered states, dream grimoires, and forbidden tomes.

978-0-7387-0832-4, 216 pp., 6 x 9   **$14.95**

To order, call 1-877-NEW-WRLD
Prices subject to change without notice
Order at Llewellyn.com 24 hours a day, 7 days a week!

Summoning Spirits
The Art of Magical Evocation
KONSTANTINOS

Summon miracles with the help of powerful spirits. Evoking a spirit is one of the most powerful magical acts you can perform. For centuries, the technique has been kept secret or revealed in unusable fragments by those with little evocation experience. *Summoning Spirits* is a complete training manual written by a practicing magician. It makes evocations easy to do, even if you've never performed a magical ritual before.

Obtain mystical abilities . . . locate hidden treasure . . . control the weather . . . even command a spirit army to protect your home while you're away! Perform evocations to both the astral and physical planes, and learn opening and banishing rituals. *Summoning Spirits* includes complete sample rituals.

978-1-56718-381-8, 240 pp., 7 x 10   **$15.95**

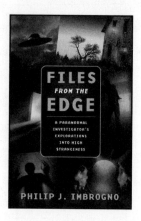

Files From the Edge

A Paranormal Investigator's Explorations
into High Strangeness

PHILIP J. IMBROGNO

Ghost lights, otherworldly creatures, visits from another dimension. The most bizarre and amazing case studies from a renowned paranormal investigator are presented here.

In his thirty-year career, Philip J. Imbrogno has researched a vast array of fascinating supernatural phenomena—the perpetually haunted mines of Putnam County, New York; encounters with strange entities at sacred megalithic stones; Bigfoot, Yeti, and other humanoids; sea creatures; psychic phenomena; the dangerous jinn; and a vast array of life forms from other worlds. The author's objective, scientific analysis—combined with credible witness testimonials and Imbrogno's own thrilling experiences—provides eye-opening, convincing evidence of our multidimensional universe.

978-0-7387-1881-1, 336 pp., 5³⁄₁₆ x 8   **$17.95**